# THE
# CONSERVATIVE
# HEART

## ALSO BY ARTHUR C. BROOKS

*The Road to Freedom:*
*How to Win the Fight for Free Enterprise*

*The Battle: How the Fight Between Free Enterprise and*
*Big Government Will Shape America's Future*

*Who Really Cares:*
*The Surprising Truth About Compassionate Conservatism*

*Gross National Happiness:*
*Why Happiness Matters for America and*
*How We Can Get More of It*

*Social Entrepreneurship:*
*A Modern Approach to Social Value Creation*

# THE CONSERVATIVE HEART

## HOW TO BUILD A FAIRER, HAPPIER, AND MORE PROSPEROUS AMERICA

## ARTHUR C. BROOKS

**BROADSIDE BOOKS**
*An Imprint of* HarperCollins*Publishers*

HarperCollins books may be purchased for educational, business, or sales promotional use. For information, please e-mail the Special Markets Department at SPsales@harpercollins.com.

FIRST EDITION

Library of Congress Cataloging-in-Publication Data

Brooks, Arthur C., 1964–
The conservative heart : a new vision for the pursuit of happiness, earned success, and social justice / Arthur C. Brooks.
        pages   cm
    Summary: "The product of years of research and analysis by Arthur Brooks that lead him to conclude what people need most are four "institutions of meaning": faith, family, community, and meaningful work. It combines reporting, original research, and case studies in a manifesto that will help people lead happier, satisfying lives"— Provided by publisher.
    ISBN 978-0-06-231975-3 (hardback) — ISBN 978-0-06-231976-0 (trade paperback) — ISBN 978-0-06-231977-7 (e-book)
1. Conservatism—United States.   2. Social values—United States.   3. Social change—United States.   I. Title.

    JC573.2.U6B77   2015
    320.520973—dc23                              2015012580

15   16   17   18   19   OV/RRD   10   9   8   7   6   5

In memory of James Q. Wilson

# CONTENTS

# THE CONSERVATIVE HEART:

## How We Have Changed the World— But Can't Seem to Get Our Footing

I remember the first time I saw real poverty. It was the early 1970s, so I would have been seven or eight years old. Flipping through a copy of *National Geographic* magazine, I found a heart-breaking photo. It showed a malnourished African boy, about my own age, with flies on his face and a distended belly.

I had never seen poverty like that before. True, by today's standards, my childhood neighborhood in Seattle would be considered pretty austere. As far as I know, my parents were the only ones in our working-class neighborhood with a college education. Some of our neighbors relied on food stamps. Most of the families were headed by a single parent. But compared to that photo in *National Geographic*, my neighborhood seemed like Beverly Hills.

The tragic image provoked two sensations in me. The first was helplessness. There was really nothing I could do for the boy, besides offering up some prayers or maybe sending my allowance to UNICEF. Even as a little kid, I grasped that anything I could personally do would be inadequate.

After helplessness came indignation. It was not *fair* that I was well fed and loved in my home in Seattle while that boy was starving to death in Africa through absolutely no fault of his own.

Of course, poverty didn't just affect children in Africa. I was born on May 21, 1964, one day before President Lyndon B. Johnson gave his famous speech announcing the Great Society. As I would learn later, it was a time of growing awareness of the crushing poverty that existed in places like Appalachia and Mississippi, as well as America's cities. We were recognizing that the poverty in our midst was an affront to our sense of fairness, and to the principle that everyone in America deserves a fair shot and a square deal. Was our domestic poverty less severe than that in Africa and India? Sure. But any poverty in a great nation like ours was a problem we had to solve.

I grew up, went to school, found a job, and started a family. But that image of the boy from *National Geographic* stayed with me. Not infrequently, I would look back and wonder, what happened to that boy? Of course, there is no way to know his specific fate. But more generally, I wondered, what happened to desperately poor people like him? Was life better or worse?

We know the answer. Poverty still exists around the world, of course. But on the whole, it has fallen dramatically since I was a kid. Consider the circumstances of the world's poorest people— those who live on a dollar a day or less, which is a traditional measure of starvation-level poverty. This percentage has fallen by 80 percent since 1970, adjusted for inflation.[1] When I was a child, more than one in four people around the world lived on that amount or less. Today, only about one in twenty live on that little. This is the greatest antipoverty achievement in world history.

So how did this remarkable transformation come to pass? Was it the fabulous success of the United Nations? The generosity of

U.S. foreign aid? The brilliant policies of the International Monetary Fund and the World Bank? Stimulus spending and government redistribution?

No, it was primarily none of those things. Billions of souls around the world have been able to pull themselves out of poverty thanks to five incredible innovations: globalization, free trade, property rights, the rule of law, and entrepreneurship. And by the way, in places like East Asia, these five things were all made possible by the historic peace after World War II that resulted from America's global diplomatic and military presence.

Back when I was a kid, when we Americans saw the world's poor, they saw us, too. We saw their poverty; they saw our freedom and our prosperity. They threw off the chains of poverty and tyranny by copying our American ways. It was the free enterprise system that not only attracted millions of the world's poor to our shores and gave them lives of dignity, but also empowered billions more worldwide to pull themselves out of poverty.

The ideals of free enterprise and global leadership, central to American conservatism, are responsible for the greatest reduction in human misery since mankind began its long climb from the swamp to the stars. This remarkable progress has been America's gift to the world.

But what about poverty right here at home? Paradoxically, here we have less reason to celebrate. To be sure, poor Americans have made material advances since I was a boy, like the rest of society. And in absolute terms, the American poor live more comfortably than poor people in the developing world. But relatively speaking, our progress in defeating poverty has been utterly substandard. While our values have been beating back poverty around the globe, the poverty rate here in America remains virtually unchanged since Lyndon Johnson's day. While American-style free enterprise has radically reduced poverty around the world, our own progress against domestic poverty has ground to a halt.

Even more paradoxically, it is precisely the loudest champions of free enterprise—the heroes of poverty relief in the developing world—who the public trusts the *least* to fight for struggling people here at home. Conservatives have the most effective solutions for human flourishing in our intellectual DNA. Our ideas have lifted up people all over the world. But the American people do not trust us to put those principles into practice to help those who need help right here.

## MY WINDING PATH TO THE RIGHT

I didn't start out as a conservative. First I was a musician, and a liberal bohemian one at that. My hometown of Seattle is one of the most progressive cities in America. And my early path made me exactly the sort of slacker that right-wingers love to make fun of. I dropped out of college at nineteen to pursue my dream of making my living in classical music. During what my parents referred to as my "gap decade," I traveled the world playing concerts, barely making my rent every month, and having a blast.

What was I pursuing? Happiness, of course. By my late twenties, I had a steady gig in the French horn section of the Barcelona Symphony Orchestra. I had moved to Spain to convince a girl named Ester to marry me—which she did. Every night in Barcelona, I got to play the greatest music ever written. On paper, I had achieved exactly what I had hoped for. I had defined happiness as the freedom to pursue my dreams to make music and travel the world, and I'd attained exactly that.

As the years went by, though, I realized that life wasn't really for me. I found myself enjoying my career less and less. Looking out a decade or two, I didn't see a lot of professional happiness in store. I figured I needed to find a new line of work before I got too much older. Unfortunately, there weren't very many options for someone without an education. This dawned on me one day as I was walking down a Barcelona street after a rehearsal. I got to thinking, What if I quit music and found a "Real Job"? (That's what we musicians called nonmusic work.) I started to do calculations in my head, based on what a guy without a college education and no practical skills could probably earn. The numbers were so grim that I started to think about going back to college.

Easier said than done, though: This was the early 1990s, well into the explosion of college costs. And for a twenty-something dropout like me, scholarship offers weren't exactly pouring in. That led me back to America, to a job teaching French horn at a small conservatory, and to Thomas Edison State College in Trenton, New Jersey, where I signed up to do an inexpensive BA entirely by correspondence.

I enrolled in courses in math, anthropology, and literature. To my utter shock, I fell in love with *economics*. I didn't know the first thing about the topic beforehand. In fact, I remembered having been forced to take one of those dumb aptitude tests in high school, which proclaimed that economics was the field to which I was *least* suited.

But as I studied it at age twenty-eight, it blew my mind at every turn. I learned that market forces tend to win out even when we don't want them to, and that good intentions are no guarantee of good results. I learned that we can't change behavior just by passing a law against something we don't like. I learned that people are complex and respond to different incentives, which is why so many social problems are not fixable through government programs. But most of all, I learned that American-style democratic capitalism was changing the world and helping billions of poor people to build their lives.

To my shock, I also learned—when sharing this newfound knowledge with my musician friends—that this outlook made me a "conservative."

That was a foreign label for me, especially because I was feeling more idealistic than ever. The more I read and learned, the more I believed that everyone—poor, rich, minority, immigrant, everyone—should be able to earn their success. I realized that free enterprise could build a better, more humane world on a mass scale, so long as the United States had the moral confidence to live its own values and share them with the world.

If all that made me a conservative, I decided, then so be it.

Little by little, I turned my career toward an exploration of these progressive "conservative" ideals. While teaching music I completed my bachelor's degree in economics. A master's degree and PhD in public policy followed, and then ten years of teaching economics and social entrepreneurship, most of them at Syracuse University. (In academia, contrary to what some readers might imagine, I never received a wedgie in the faculty lounge on account of my conservative views. My colleagues treated me with unfailing kindness and respect.)

At Syracuse I taught one or two classes a semester and spent the balance of my time on research. My research was fun, but some of it was, well, esoteric. One of my articles, published in the *Journal of Public Economic Theory* (you don't subscribe?), was titled "Genetic Algorithms and Public Economics." Another one that didn't exactly go onto the bestseller list was "Contingent Valuation and the Winner's Curse in Internet Art Auctions."

But the main part of my research was dedicated to two things that almost everyone cares about: charity and happiness. In both cases, I found a startling correlation with political ideology. First, I found that conservatives give more to charity than liberals do, even after correcting for income differences. Much of this difference is due to the fact that conservatives are more religious than liberals, on average, but it still struck me as surprising. Second, I found in self-reported survey data that conservatives are—on average—happier than liberals.

This finding generated a lot of attention. The notion that political conservatives had a happiness edge on their rivals proved to be controversial, especially given the stereotype that conservatives are hard-hearted disciplinarians who disdain anything touchy-feely. This was not the result I'd expected to find. But the data defied my expectations.

During these years, I wasn't just a student of happiness. I did my best to walk the walk in my own life. Every year on my birthday, I resolved to examine my life and intentionally try to sketch the next ten years of my pursuit of happiness. When I turned forty, I couldn't deny that most things were going great. I had a terrific marriage, three kids, and an academic career I adored. But something was missing: impact. I remembered the kid in the *National Geographic*, and I saw the people right here in America who were still missing the blessings of the free enterprise system in their lives. I wondered how I could use my newfound skills and passions in the service of these people. I realized that my own pursuit of happiness required that I join the fight to make the pursuit of happiness possible for more of my fellow citizens.

So I set a goal for myself. By the time I turned fifty, I wanted to be a scholar at the American Enterprise Institute (AEI), the highest temple of the conservative intellectual movement. AEI is a Washington, D.C., think tank started in 1938. It houses some of America's finest scholars and serves the needs of the nation's policymakers. Imagine an idea laboratory full of mad public policy scientists and you get a rough picture. If I wanted to do work that really helped people, I figured, that's where I'd be best able to do it.

Turns out I only had to wait until I was forty-four. Proving that the free enterprise system makes almost anything possible, this onetime college dropout and footloose musician became AEI's eleventh president on January 1, 2009, three weeks before the inauguration of President Barack Obama.

Just a few months earlier, the near collapse of the economy had sent America into an economic tailspin and ensured that issues of poverty, social mobility, and rising economic inequality would be the defining issues of our time. It also led to widespread denunciation of capitalism itself. A populist movement arose that demanded greater regulation of the economy, higher taxes, more redistributive spending—all the things that we conservatives opposed.

As longtime defenders of capitalism, conservatives had been put on the defensive. For the past 20 years, our movement had basked in the glow of capitalism's victory over the socialist alternative. But now, it seemed to many that the weaknesses in our economic status quo had finally come home to roost.

How would conservatives respond to the crisis of American free enterprise? The answer would in large part be determined by our work at AEI.

## THE CONSERVATIVE PARADOX

Taking the helm at AEI, I spent most of my time fund-raising. The institute has a policy of accepting zero funding from the government and receives all its support from private donations. But I was also thrust into the middle of the hottest political debates in Washington. In addition to voluminous research, events, and media appearances, AEI works directly with top policymakers on a regular basis. For example, we host regular debate training and messaging seminars for members of Congress, an activity in which I became deeply involved. I saw up close exactly how their minds work and how they argued their policies. At the beginning,

I would go home and excitedly tell Ester whom I had met that day. Like a little kid, I'd report, "I actually had lunch with Senator So-and-So!"

"That's great," she would reply with typical Spanish sarcasm. "Is he dreamy?"

Sometimes I'm asked whether my faith in our leaders went up or down when I started working closely with the politicians we all see on TV. Readers might be surprised to learn that my estimation of these men and women actually went up—a lot. It is easy to be cynical about politicians. We live in an age in which tearing down the high and mighty has become a twisted type of public sport. But being a member of Congress (or running for president) is a crushing job. The cognitive demands are intense, the travel is punitive, and the personal attacks are relentless. It's hard to understand why someone would seek these jobs. Yet they do, and not for exorbitant pay, either. Some just love the perks and power, I suppose. But I can say after getting to know many quite well that most do it because they truly love their country.

By the time the novelty of working with politicians wore off, I was able to focus on the problems they were facing, especially those of the conservatives. They faced what I came to call the "Conservative Paradox."

If conservative ideals have done so much to lift up the poor around the world, you would think the conservative movement would be gaining strength every single day. And not just gaining strength among wealthy people or Americans with traditional moral values, but also among young idealists, immigrants, minorities, and advocates for the poor—all embracing a new conservative movement and unleashing its power on behalf of America's most vulnerable!

Unless you have been living in a cave, you know that this is *not* what has happened. To the contrary, the conservative movement is struggling to attract new followers, and indeed some believe it will ultimately go the way of social democratic Europe's conservative remnant.

What explains this discrepancy between the incredible results of free enterprise in the developing world, the continued stagnation of poor communities in America, and the political unpopularity of conservatives in so many quarters? One answer is simple: The defenders of free enterprise have done a terrible job of telling people how much good the system has done around the world. According to a 2013 survey, 84 percent of Americans are unaware that worldwide deprivation has fallen as dramatically as it has over the past three decades. Indeed, more than two-thirds actually think global hunger has actually gotten worse, in direct contradiction of all the facts.[2] Capitalism has saved a couple of billion people and we have treated this miracle like a state secret.

But there's more to it than just ignorance. Millions of Americans believe the American Dream is no longer within their reach and that conservatives don't care. Millions of Americans don't see the benefits of democratic capitalism extending to them, their families, and the poor. Millions of Americans no longer believe that their children will be better off than they had been. And millions of Americans see conservatives as oblivious to these problems.

This is a crisis of confidence in American exceptionalism—and in American conservatism.


When my mother's grandparents first came steaming into New York Harbor from Denmark in 1890, they were risking everything to get to a country where everyone—even uneducated and poor people like them—could earn success. And earn their success they did. After a few years, they owned their own farm in South

Dakota. They never made much money, but they built their own lives, raised twelve kids, worshipped God freely, and lived to a ripe old age.

Most people have a similar family story. Virtually none of us come from landed gentry; we're basically a country of outcasts. Even the descendants of the *Mayflower* and the Daughters of the American Revolution come from a line of European riffraff with nowhere to go but up.

That's why mobility is such a big part of the American Dream. Other countries have castes, peasant classes, permanent haves and have-nots. By contrast, America's culture is supposed to be one of abundant opportunity. As far as I know, my great-grandfather didn't arrive here, look around, and say with a sigh, "Well, I guess I'll be low man on the totem pole from now on." But neither did he proclaim, "Sure is great to be in America, where I can get a fairer system of forced income redistribution!" He was here for freedom and opportunity. He was here to be measured by his merit and hard work.

People still want this. But the shadow of pessimism is growing. Many ordinary Americans are convinced that our unique culture of opportunity and mobility is disappearing—that one of our country's unique strengths is evaporating.

Every year, Gallup asks a large sample of Americans, "In general, are you satisfied or dissatisfied with the way things are going in the United States at this time?"[3] In December 2000, 46 percent said they were dissatisfied—already depressingly high. By December 2014, six years into the Obama administration's plan to create a fairer and more compassionate nation, the percentage had shot up to 76 percent.

You read that right. Three in four Americans are dissatisfied with the United States.

What happened? It's not that there's more crime. There isn't.

It's not that people are dying younger. In fact, they're living longer and with better health.

The problem is that Americans have come to think the game is rigged and the American Dream isn't available to everyone. The basic bargain in America is supposed to be that no matter where you start out, if you work hard and play by the rules, you can make out all right. Maybe you won't get rich, but you can "pursue your happiness," in the formulation of the Founders, and build a life of independence and dignity.

But people look around today, and what do they see? Poor Americans may be better off than poor Africans, but they are *staying* poor. In the wake of the Great Recession, an asymmetric recovery has cleaved the country into winners and losers like never before. Work has disappeared for those at the bottom; government dependency has grown; mobility has fallen. Meanwhile, the rich have gotten richer, with most of the income growth of the past seven years flowing to the wealthiest Americans.

Even the middle class feels left out. People see corporate cronies getting rich because of their cozy relationship with the government. They see bailouts for huge banks but small businesses going bust. They see government loan guarantees for big companies with friends in high places, but hear "No loans for you" from their local bank.

Here is a perfect summation of our national pessimism, uttered in December 2013:

> *The American people's frustration . . . is rooted in their own daily battles to make ends meet . . . the nagging sense that no matter how hard they work, the deck is stacked against them . . . the fear that their kids won't be better off than they were . . . and lack of upward mobility that has jeopardized middle class America's basic bargain: that if you work hard, you have a chance to get ahead.*

Who do you think said this? A right-wing critic of the current administration? A political aspirant for president, scoring layups against the mediocre performance of the economy during President Obama's tenure?

No, it comes from President Obama himself.

How ironic. While branding itself the protector of the little guy—the "99 percent"—the administration has not helped the most vulnerable. America has effectively been split in two, with poor people falling farther and farther behind.

I will back this up with plenty of evidence in the coming chapters. But for now, suffice it to say that the administration's ostensibly pro-poor, tough-on-the-wealthy agenda has actually made things worse. Today, there is unprecedented opportunity and prosperity for those at the top. But at the bottom, the chance to work, rise, and earn success is disappearing.


But if the American Dream is fading for millions under the current administration, why aren't Americans turning to conservatives for better solutions?

Simple: People don't think conservatives care. One recent poll found that 56 percent of Americans say they believe the word *compassionate* describes the Republican Party "not at all well," versus 5 percent who say it describes the party "very well."[4] If you take elected Republicans, paid staff, and blood relatives out of that last number, it probably rounds to about zero.

Where did Americans get this idea? From their own ears, that's where.

When Americans listen to the right, they hear us talk endlessly about debt, deficits, taxes, spending, and fiscal responsibility—and conclude that all we care about is money. They hear conservative politicians declare that the only thing you need to get ahead in America is a willingness to work hard—and they conclude we are out of touch. They hear some Republican leaders characterize people at the bottom as moochers—and conclude we do not care about their struggles. They hear us rail against "big government"— and conclude we just want to lower tax rates for billionaires.

The political left has failed in its fight for the poor, and not just during this administration. The failure goes back many decades. But truthfully, there has been little alternative coming from the political right. Too often, the right has failed even to acknowledge the problems of poverty and unequal opportunity. And so, when the president utters words that effectively indict his own policies, there's no real reaction.

Progressives in America have always insisted that we focus our attention on the plight of the poor and vulnerable. I admire them for speaking up. However, as I will show in the chapters that follow, they have failed in that fight because they misdiagnose the problem struggling Americans face. They often treat work as a punishment, view struggling people as liabilities to manage, and focus on unequal distribution of incomes instead of unequal and insufficient opportunity. As a result, progressive politicians try to help the poor with government redistribution programs that frequently exacerbate the problem. These intrusions lower opportunity, reduce our ability to create actual private-sector work, leave more people dependent on the state, and effectively split the country into two Americas even more quickly.

If we conservatives were as smart as we think we are, our movement would have already seized on this as a tremendous moral and political opportunity. "Look," we might say, "the other guys have made the poor worse off. That's immoral!" Stunningly, however, we don't do that.

Instead, most voices on the American right have failed to acknowledge that there is a crisis of poverty and insufficient opportunity—that we are, in some respects, two Americas. And even when conservatives do acknowledge this, many often discuss the problem in ways that alienate the American people by implying that those who are struggling just don't want to work hard.

When people find out that I run AEI, they often begin venting their frustrations with Washington. I cannot count how many conversations have boiled down to the same basic conclusion. When many people assess the political landscape, they see two choices: a heartless, pragmatic party on the right and an imprudent but compassionate party on the left. Americans are good people, so given that rotten choice, compassion almost always wins. That's especially true in times of hardship. So the political right loses—and, more importantly, vulnerable Americans are left with almost no one in Washington who both projects empathy for their struggles and proposes policies that will actually attack the root causes of those struggles.

Conservatives are in possession of the best solutions to the problems of poverty and economic mobility. Yet because we don't speak in a way that reflects our hearts, many Americans simply don't trust us and are unwilling to give us the chance to implement those solutions. They know instinctively that outmoded redistributionist arguments generally yield lousy results, but they feel they have no palatable alternative. And so the poor might not starve, but they are staying poor. That is simply unacceptable.


I believe that poverty and opportunity are moral issues and must be addressed as such.

Some of my fellow conservatives are hesitant to accept this. I hear pretty frequently that we should focus on economics and not morality. That is dead wrong and a false choice besides. Economic issues *are* moral issues. Americans are not materialists. The vast majority of Americans want public policies that are not merely economically efficient, but also morally just. Lifting vulnerable people up and giving everyone a chance to earn success is primarily a matter of compassion and fairness. And approximately 100 percent of Americans care about these things. As New York University social psychologist Jonathan Haidt has shown, virtually everybody—right and left, young and old, religious and non-religious—has "moral taste buds" that crave the universal values of compassion and fairness.[5]

So when conservatives fail to invoke compassion and fairness in our bid to solve society's problems, we preemptively surrender arguments with near-total support from the public. That's insane. If conservatives want to become a true majority movement and unite the nation in a way that lifts up everyone, then we need to build our message around majoritarian values. Compassion and fairness are majoritarian values.

We need to learn from self-identified liberals, who encompass just a quarter of the population but boldly claim to fight for the "99 percent." Progressives understand that minorities fight against things while majorities fight for people. Even though they are the political minority, they see themselves as a majoritarian social movement that aims to fundamentally transform America. And they are succeeding, because conservatives have ceded the moral high ground and contented themselves with railing against the terrible things the left is doing to America.

That needs to change. The time has come for the American right to reclaim the moral high ground and transform itself from a protest movement into a social movement. We need to stop focusing just on what we are against and boldly proclaim what we stand *for*. We need to put forward a hopeful, optimistic governing agenda—one that focuses on improving the lives of all people, especially the most vulnerable, through authentically conservative policies. And if we want to win elections so we can do all this, we must remember how to speak in a way that reflects the moral bedrock of our cause.

We must build a social movement that is dedicated to ensuring every citizen's opportunity, regardless of his or her station in life, to pursue happiness and earn success. We must deputize every American as a hero on behalf of others who are being left behind. We must make our coalition the undisputed moral champion of fairness and compassion in American politics.

This absolutely does not mean that we must shift leftward or soften our convictions. To the contrary, we must show the American people a new vision of compassion and fairness that is written on the conservative heart.

## WHAT IS WRITTEN ON THE CONSERVATIVE HEART?

The sad truth is that millions of Americans today think conservatives are oblivious to the struggles of their everyday lives. That has to change if we want to see our movement truly ascendant. But before we explore how to do that, let's spend a moment reflecting on what most conservatives truly believe about helping others. Forget how we are portrayed in the media; forget how we clumsily cast ourselves in public debates. Here's what my experience as a social scientist, my years at the helm of AEI, and my daily interaction with all sorts of Americans tell me is written on the conservative heart.

There is a common misconception that conservatives are materialistic. We are not, and this confusion is a central political irony of our time. Progressives truly want to help the poor but have tried to solve poverty primarily with government money, relegating talk of culture to the past and focusing more and more on income inequality. The obsession with redistribution for its own sake comes skillfully wrapped in the moral language of fairness and compassion. This is materialism tarted up to look like moralism.

On the other hand, though conservatives often wrap our arguments in lackluster materialistic language about tax rates and GDP growth, our philosophy takes a uniquely holistic view of human dignity, the conditions of earned success and human flourishing. The conservative heart rebels against the modern world's siren song that instructs us to love things and use people. We know that human dignity has deeper roots than the financial resources someone commands. We may wear the rhetorical uniform of materialists, but conservatives at heart are moralists.

Moral hope, not lust for wealth, is the reason conservatives delight in entrepreneurialism and classic American success stories. President Obama, of course, spoke extensively of "hope" in 2008. But many Americans believe this turned out to be a hollow promise—little more than a chimera wrapped in government help for people struggling to get by.

It is conservatives who stand for *true* hope, a hope that returns power and agency back into the hands of ordinary people. We extol free enterprise, self-reliance, and ethical living—the foundations of a good life, no matter how much money someone makes.

And what about the role of government in helping the needy? Contrary to what we often hear, the vast majority of conservatives agree with the great libertarian economist Friedrich Hayek and President Ronald Reagan that the social safety net for truly indigent people is a great achievement of modern civilization.

Ironically, one key reason we so often fight to limit government is that fiscal profligacy actually poses a massive threat to the social safety net. Conservatives know that only a return to fiscal conservatism can guarantee the solvency of the safety net, and ensure that full-blown austerity will never inflict massive pain on those who can least afford to bear it. Because we believe in a true safety net, we must protect it with fiscal discipline. There is no other way.

What is more, traditional conservatism is the only way to make the safety net unnecessary for the most people. Only a culture of opportunity, fueled with a policy agenda of education reform, private job creation, and entrepreneurship, can truly set people up to flourish.

So why do conservatives so often complain about the safety net? Because as it is currently administered, it does not equip citizens to build meaningful dignified lives of their own making. The conservative heart demands more for the poor than subsistence and dependence. As a result, conservatives define success by how few people need help from government programs, not how many we can enroll for government help. We have seen how the number of Americans on federal nutritional assistance ("food stamps") has skyrocketed in recent years. Some look at those figures and see great success. They say, "Hey, look! We helped all these people! Isn't that fantastic?" But conservatives in touch with their hearts will reply with incredulity: "We have sixty-some percent more people on food stamps five years after the end of the recession than we had at the beginning? That isn't success. It is failure."

Conservatives understand that there is nothing soft about true compassion. Real compassion is steely-edged, hard-core stuff. True compassion means telling a friend, "I can't help you if you don't stop using drugs," or, "I can't help you if you won't pay child support." It means only helping people who are ready to help themselves. And when they are ready, it means providing genuine support that effectively addresses the whole person.

While we sometimes express ourselves poorly, ours is not a worldview that sees poor people as liabilities to be managed. Conservatives fundamentally view poor people as dormant assets to be enlivened. The poor are not a burden on society in need only of charity. They are an untapped source of strength and growth, so long as we have the optimism and confidence to help them as they build their lives. Charity is important, but what poor men and women really need is *investment*. That's why conservatives insist on work as the central solution to poverty, and why work is so central to this book. As I will explain in depth, there are two kinds of people in the world: those who think work is a punishment and those who see work as a blessing.

The conservative heart is emphatically in the second camp. That is why we admire hard work, admonish people who slack off, and support policies such as work requirements for welfare. We understand that when society empowers people to work for social assistance, we help those people twice. First, through welfare, we are helping meet their immediate material needs. And second, through work, we are helping them earn success—the key to a fulfilling and dignified life.

Earned success, by the way, is also what we believe people *want*. People naturally feel dissatisfied with simply having things given to them for free. It is the mission of the conservative movement— the very reason of our existence—to make it possible for every single American to earn his or her own way.

But the blessings of work go far beyond the alleviation of poverty. Conservatives know—and must argue tirelessly—that meaningful work is not limited to jobs that pay a lot and require college degrees. Everyone who creates value, from venture capitalists to landscapers to stay-at-home moms, is engaged in meaningful work of transcendent value. Conservatives know this, and contrary to caricatures, most grasp that most people who are falling behind are not doing so on purpose. The core problem is not that too many people are "taking" public support, but that too many lack a real opportunity to "make" a living. The changing structure of the American economy, the Great Recession, and the policies of recent years have all conspired to keep these people down. Our job as conservatives is to champion them.

In my travels across the country, I have encountered thousands of conservative activists. And what has impressed me over and over is how deeply their principles and actions are rooted in a passion for America and a desire to make this country what it should be—a land of opportunity, an exceptional nation where anyone can get ahead through hard work and determination, a place where our origins matter less than our destinations, a beacon of hope and opportunity for all the world. This is what America has been, and can be again.

Restoring that America—that is what animates the conservative heart.


I know what some readers are probably asking. Is this description of the conservative heart just "compassionate conservatism," the old concept from a few presidential campaigns ago?

No. Setting aside a host of policy problems, even the phrase "compassionate conservatism" is problematic. It validates those who falsely claim that conservatives are uncompassionate in the first place. It grafts "compassion" onto conservatism like an unnatural appendage. This is a major error. Notwithstanding our communication failures, a creed that flows from the optimistic belief that every person is valuable and capable of earned success is inherently compassionate to the core.

Here's what a truly uncompassionate worldview would look like: It would throw in the towel on people and whole communities. It would lazily presume that a certain segment of the population simply can't make it, that they require an unending stream of unsatisfying government support to grind along at subsistence levels. A movement built on free enterprise, real hope, and earned success sees right through this lazy nihilism—and rejects it.

No, we should never endorse the myth that "compassion" is a new idea for conservatives. That is why I have titled this book *The Conservative Heart*. There is no adjunct to the conservative heart. No qualifiers. No hyphenation. Our objective is not to soften conservatism's rough edges or erode away its principles. It is not to agitate for "big government conservatism" or to shill for the same old statist machinery with a slightly different set of management consultants at the controls.

Our goal is to explain to the world what is really written on the conservative heart. It is to reclaim the mantles of compassion and fairness for the movement that truly lives up to them, to make the pursuit of happiness a reality for every single American, and to dramatically rethink public policy so the blessings of work and opportunity can reach people who are being left behind.

## THE ROAD AHEAD

In 1953, when Russell Kirk published *The Conservative Mind*, conservatives were widely dismissed as anti-intellectual reactionaries. As one prominent progressive thinker put it at the time, conservatives were only capable of "irritable mental gestures which seek to resemble ideas."[6] Kirk unmasked this lie. He showed that modern conservatism was built on a rich philosophical tradition stretching back at least two centuries to the writings of the English philosopher and statesman Edmund Burke.

Today, thanks to Kirk and other conservative intellectuals, Americans no longer doubt the rigor of the conservative mind. What they do doubt is the compassion of the conservative heart. The time has come to correct this false perception, and to unite conservative mind and heart behind a new social movement to restore the promise of America for every one of our citizens.

In the chapters ahead, I will explain how we can build this new conservative social movement. We will reveal the secrets to real human happiness. We will examine how these secrets have been denied to millions of Americans through misbegotten government policies and misdirected culture. And we will learn to share humanistic conservatism in a way that opens minds and rallies people to our cause. (If you are in a hurry, you can turn to the last chapter, which provides the seven secrets to communicating all the ideas in this book.)

There will be plenty of data along the way, along with a lot of colorful characters. We will meet neuroscientists, homeless men, senators, billionaires, and a penniless Hindu swami. All of them will help us understand what we believe and how to share it with others.

As we embark on our journey, we will discover that what America needs most of all is not a magical set of new laws. Nor is it, for that matter, mere repeal of bad policies or the replacement of many elected leaders—though both might do a world of good. What the United States needs is for a unifying, positive, aspirational force to sweep through our national community. American conservatives have a generational opportunity to become precisely this kind of force. We have a shot, if we take it, to help every single American build a better life, and unite our nation in the process.

This is a book, to be sure, for committed conservatives who are hungry to improve our movement. But it is more than a mere political road map for one side of the aisle. I write not just for "true believers," but also for ideologically unaligned and disaffected Americans who see little from either side that inspires them. And just as sincerely, this is a book for open-minded liberals who understand that our country would benefit from new passion and new ideas in the fight against poverty.

In short, *The Conservative Heart* is a book about human flourishing for freethinkers of all stripes. It is a book for everyone who feels a moral obligation to give every American a better shot at living a happy and meaningful life.

# Chapter 1

# AMERICA'S PURSUIT OF HAPPINESS:

## Why It Is the Central Expression of the Conservative Heart

W here does our exploration of the conservative heart start? [1] When asked how to lift people up, many—especially in Washington D.C.—turn directly to policy products: taxes, spending, or the safety net. But this is not the right starting point, not because these things don't matter but rather because they are mere tools. Even jobs and economic growth, which we often mistake for our fundamental goals, are actually just instrumental things. We need to go much deeper to find something that speaks to us with true, intrinsic importance. Something that all of us want, and that links everyone together as people.

Fortunately, we know where to look. America's Founders clearly explained our nation's moral purpose in the country's mission statement. The Declaration of Independence defines the very center of the American experiment—the coin of the realm—as none other than the *pursuit of happiness*.

In the Declaration, Thomas Jefferson insisted that this journey toward a meaningful life is as important as life and liberty. He proclaimed that it is an unalienable right for everyone. And he avowed that this right comes directly from God. Decades after he drafted the Declaration, Jefferson explained its contents as "an expression of the American mind."[2] More accurately, I believe, the pursuit of happiness was an expression of the American *heart*. And it must be the central expression of the conservative heart today. Why?

First, the pursuit of happiness is being foreclosed to too many Americans due to misguided policy and a hostile culture. When conservatives complain about "big government," for example, they are really angry about the intrusion of the state into people's lives and the soul-crushing dependency it often creates—both of which are incompatible with the pursuit of happiness. When conservatives complain about a culture that is increasingly hostile to values like hard work and family formation, they are actually angry that the happiness that comes from those institutions is being denied to the people—the poor and young—who need them most.

Second, to take on these challenges, we must not only be warriors for those who need us—we must be *happy* warriors. There is a lot to be mad about in America today, but we must never forget that our cause is a joyous one. Conservatives should be optimists who believe in people. We champion hope and opportunity. Fighting for people, helping those who need us, and saving the country—this is, and should be, happy work.

In sum, our Founders believed that happiness was at the center of the American experiment; the pursuit of happiness eludes too many Americans today; and the conservative heart should be a happy heart.

So happiness is where we start our journey to build better lives for everyone.

## THE HAPPINESS PORTFOLIO

How happy are you, on a scale of 1 to 10? Perhaps it sounds crazy to measure it in this way, but psychologists and economists who study happiness have been doing it for years. The richest data available come from the University of Chicago's General Social Survey, a survey of Americans conducted since 1972.

Researchers believe these results are accurate and believable, and the numbers on happiness are surprisingly consistent over time. In surveys taken every other year for four decades, roughly one-third of Americans have said they're "very happy." About half report being "pretty happy." And only about 10 to 15 percent typically say they're "not too happy."[3]

Now, these averages conceal some interesting differences. For many years, researchers found that women were happier than men, though the gap may now be closing.[4] Typically, single women are happier than single men; married women are happier than married men; and widowed women are happier than widowed men. (My wife was distressingly unsurprised by that last point.)

It turns out that conservative women are particularly blissful: about 40 percent say they are very happy.[5] That makes them slightly happier than conservative men and significantly happier than liberal women. The unhappiest are liberal men, only about one-fifth of whom consider themselves very happy.

But as any of us can attest, two people who are almost identical on paper will not likely have identical happiness. We cannot predict our life satisfaction from how we would fill out the census. That's where an understanding of our three crucial *sources* of happiness comes in.

The first key source of happiness is our genes. In one particularly fascinating genre of research, scholars track and study the lives of identical twins who were separated as infants and raised by separate families.[6] By examining these genetic carbon copies who were brought up in different environments, these "twin studies" help us disentangle nature from nurture.

And when these studies look at the twins' happiness, they arrive at a surprising result. Frankly, if you're as obsessed as I am with the idea of building your own life, you might find it a little unsettling. That's because a whopping proportion—about 48 percent—of our general sense of well-being at any given moment seems to be driven by our genetic makeup.[7] When you blame unhappiness on your parents, you're actually half right!

The second major driver of happiness is the events that inflect our lives—the big, one-off things, good and bad. Landing your dream job, opening an acceptance letter to a great college, being left at the altar, or having a bad accident. Studies suggest that these kinds of events do control a big fraction of our happiness—up to roughly 40 percent at any given time.[8]

If that 40 percent of happiness were permanent, then the secret to happiness would be clear. It would be all about—as so many self-improvement gurus teach—setting and reaching huge goals. "Think of the things that would thrill you, and strive for them!" That's all we'd need to know.

But that isn't enough, because the impact of each particular event proves remarkably short-lived. Imagine this 40 percent as a moving window that extends about six months into your future. If you move to a sunny place, land a big promotion, or watch your beloved team win the World Series, you will indeed get a happiness bump. But expect it to fade—and fast. If you move to California, you'll be happier because of the weather—for a few months. After that, you'll mostly just get to enjoy high taxes, a crushing mortgage, and a lot of time sitting in traffic wondering why you left Cleveland.

Now, this fact isn't really so bad. This moving window also fuels our resilience, helping us bounce back from past trauma. In one remarkable and famous study, researchers looked at two seemingly opposite groups: lottery winners and paraplegics.[9] They found that six months after winning, the lottery winners' present happiness was, for all practical purposes, indistinguishable from a control group. What's more, the winners reported deriving less pleasure from the mundane events of everyday life than either the control group or the accident victims. And finally, when all three groups were asked to project their future happiness, it was the paraplegics whose replies were the highest!

You may find this incredible. You may even think, I would rather die than lose all my mobility. No, you wouldn't. If this happened to you, eventually you would be *you* again. You are not the sum of your outward circumstances. That's a beautiful and encouraging thing.

So the news isn't all bad. But this does impose an important limitation. It means that betting on events to make us happy is a really bad strategy. The act of striving toward huge goals is worthwhile on its own, as we'll see. But the achievements themselves? Very few one-off accomplishments permanently boost happiness. The secret to flourishing is emphatically not grabbing the biggest brass ring you can find. Indeed, in a moment I will show that this strategy can even raise your *un*happiness.

Forty-eight percent of happiness is genetic. About 40 percent is current events. That leaves just 12 percent of our happiness left. That might not sound like much. But we can—and must—bring that 12 percent under our control.

Nothing has illustrated this more clearly for me than how a friend of mine handled some terrible news. We were in our mid-thirties, both newly minted PhDs, when he returned from the doctor with a devastating diagnosis. He had a congenital heart defect that had no known cure at the time. He was given about fifteen years to live.

My friend did indeed die two years ago, at age fifty. How did he spend his last decade and a half? He didn't sit at home moping around or become depressed, though that certainly would have been understandable. Instead, he decided to fit the forty-five years he thought he had into the fifteen years he actually did have. It was the most amazing thing I had ever seen. He said, "I'm going to be a better husband, a better father, a better professor, and a better citizen." He felt a duty to become better at everything he cared about—and fast. One day he apparently came home from work with an epiphany to share with his wife: "We've never been to Istanbul! It's time to go." And they went.

How many of us have a place we've always wanted to visit with a loved one? How many of us will get around to going? Well, he did. He and his wife decided they wanted more kids—and they had them. He wrung more life out of those fifteen years than most of us find in four times that long. He seized control of his happiness.

My friend's situation is actually the same as all of ours. We control about 12 percent of our happiness. We'd better not waste any of it. And here's some good news: We are in fact in control of that 12 percent. Not the government, not rich people—*we are*.

And even better news is that we know how to do it. It's about maximizing the four values that are most correlated with happiness. Call them the "happiness portfolio." They are *faith, family, community,* and *meaningful work.* To pursue these things is to pursue happiness.

The first three are fairly uncontroversial. Scholarly evidence that faith, family, and friendships increase happiness and meaning is as abundant as it is unsurprising. No one sighs regretfully on his deathbed and says, "I can't believe I wasted all that time with my wife and kids," "volunteering at the soup kitchen," or "growing in my spirituality." No one ever says, "I should have spent more time watching TV and playing Angry Birds on my phone." In my own life, nothing has given my life more meaning and satisfaction than my Catholic faith and the love of my family.

Work, though, seems less intuitive. Many people assume that even if they like their own job—whether it's market work, volunteer work, or staying at home with kids—others probably don't like theirs. According to popular culture, our jobs are pure drudgery. We all love to laugh at *Dilbert* and *The Office*. There are probably days when all of us can sympathize with the characters in the great 1999 comedy *Office Space* who ritualistically destroy their archenemy, a workplace printer, with a baseball bat.

Yet surprisingly, when researchers actually ask Americans how they like their jobs, more than 50 percent say that, all things considered, they are "completely satisfied" or "very satisfied" with their work. And when we include "fairly satisfied" the number rises to over 80 percent.[10] This is not an artifact of education level or job prestige. It doesn't matter if they went to college or not. It doesn't matter if they make above- or below-average income. The hedge fund manager and the hedge trimmer are equally likely to say they like their work.

And a love for work helps lead to a love for life. My own statistical analysis finds that Americans who feel they are successful at work are twice as likely to say they are very happy overall as people who don't feel that way.[11]

This isn't about the money. True, when people are starving or struggling, having more money relieves pressure from everyday life in tangible ways. It erases painful choices, such as having to choose between paying the rent and getting enough to eat. But here's the catch: It turns out that after those pressures are relieved, the happiness gains that more money buys level off. Once people reach a little beyond the average middle-class income level, research shows that even big financial gains don't yield much—if any—increases in happiness.[12] Indeed, focusing on money per se brings misery. (More on that in a moment.)

The happiness rewards from work are not from the money, but from the value created in our lives and in the lives of others—value that is acknowledged and rewarded. That is what we call *earned success*. President Franklin Roosevelt had it right: "Happiness lies not in the mere possession of money; it lies in the joy of achievement, in the thrill of creative effort." The secret to happiness is earned success through honest work.

When Frederick Douglass rhapsodized about "patient, enduring, honest, unremitting and indefatigable work, into which the whole heart is put," he was talking about earned success. It is central to the American ideal—a concept we inherited from our forefathers.

People grasp this intrinsically. Nearly three-quarters of Americans say they wouldn't quit their jobs even if a financial windfall enabled them to live in luxury for the rest of their lives. In a stunning twist, those with the least education, the lowest incomes, and the least prestigious jobs were actually the most likely to say they would keep working even if they didn't have to.[13] It is the elites who are comparatively likelier to say they would take the money and run.

The converse relationship between work and happiness is also true, by the way: A lack of work means a lack of happiness. We will explore the devastating blow that joblessness deals to human dignity in a later chapter. But here's a preview: When people lose their jobs, even if government aid relieves the pressures of a lost paycheck, unemployment proves totally catastrophic for happiness.[14] Research suggests, for example, that joblessness increases rates of divorce and suicide and even amplifies the severity of disease.[15]

It bears repeating that earned success is often totally uncorrelated with amassed wealth. You can measure your earned success in any currency you choose. You can count it in dollars, if you like. But you can also count it in kids taught to read, habitats protected, or souls saved. When I taught graduate students, the social entrepreneurs who pursued nonprofit careers were some of my happiest graduates. They made less money than many of their business school classmates, but they were no less certain that they were earning their success. They defined that success in nonmonetary terms and delighted in it.

To sum up so far, to pursue the happiness within our reach, we do best to pour ourselves into faith, family, community, and earned success through work. This is our happiness portfolio.

And you know what? That kind of sounds like a conservative manifesto.

## A FORMULA TO REMEMBER

Maybe you're thinking I skipped over money and related earthly rewards—fame, power, sex, and so on—a little too quickly. After all, if they weren't a big deal for happiness, people wouldn't be killing themselves and others all day long to get them, right?

Fine. Let's go to Spain and meet a man who can help us clear up that question.

Abd-ar-Rahman III was born in 891 AD. He became the emir of Cordoba in his early twenties and spent the next five decades becoming one of the most powerful rulers of his time. He built incredible palaces and stunning mosques. He raised a powerful navy, subdued rebellions, and consolidated Muslim power in Spain that lasted for centuries. He grew so powerful that he was able to claim the title caliph—leader of all Muslims in the world.

This absolute ruler lived in opulence and luxury. It is said that his harem included six thousand women.[16] In terms of money, power, fame, and pleasure, nothing was denied him. He must have been in bliss, right? Here is his own testimony:

> *I have now reigned above fifty years in victory or peace; beloved by my subjects, dreaded by my enemies, and respected by my allies. Riches and honors, power and pleasure, have waited on my call, nor does any earthly blessing appear to have been wanting to my felicity.*

Sounds great, right? Ah, but hold on. Abd-ar-Rahman continued his thought:

> *In this situation, I have diligently numbered the days of pure and genuine happiness which have fallen to my lot: They amount to fourteen.[17]*

Fourteen happy days for the richest, most powerful man in the world? Actually, Abd-ar-Rahman's problem wasn't actually happiness, despite what he believed. It was *un*happiness.

Does that sound like a distinction without a difference? If so, you probably have the same problem as the great emir, and a lot of people today. But with a little knowledge, we all can avoid the misery that befell him, and help others do so as well.

What is unhappiness, exactly? You might intuit that it is simply the opposite of happiness, just as darkness is the absence of light. That is actually not right. Happiness and unhappiness are certainly related, but are not really opposites.

Images of the brain show that parts of the left cerebral cortex are more active than the right when we are experiencing happiness, while the right side becomes more active when we are unhappy. They are distinct phenomena. So, as strange as it seems, being happier than average does not mean one can't also be unhappier than average. One common test for both happiness and unhappiness is called the PANAS (Positive and Negative Affect Schedule). I took it myself, and you can, too.[18] I found that, for happiness, I am at the top for people my age, sex, occupation, and education group. But I get a pretty high score for unhappiness as well. It turns out I am a cheerful melancholic.

So when people express dissatisfaction with their lives, whether they realize it or not, they are really doing sums. They are basically saying, "My happiness is X, my unhappiness is Y, and Y is greater than X." That compels us to take up a new question. If avoiding unhappiness isn't the same as pursuing happiness, how *can* we avoid it?

If you ask an unhappy person why he is unhappy, he'll almost always blame circumstance. In many cases, of course, this is justified. Some people are oppressed, poor, or have physical ailments that make life a chore. Research unsurprisingly finds that racism causes unhappiness in children.[19] Many academic studies trace a clear link between unhappiness and poverty.[20]

There are smaller circumstantial sources of unhappiness, too. Researchers at Princeton found that the number-one most unhappiness-provoking event in a typical day is spending time with one's boss.[21] (As a boss, this was not welcome news for me.)

So circumstances certainly play some role. No doubt Abd-ar-Rahman could have pointed to a few in his own life. But paradoxically, a better explanation for his unhappiness may have been his own quest for satisfaction—a mistaken quest eerily similar to what the modern world offers us today.

Have you ever known an alcoholic? They generally drink to relieve craving or anxiety—in other words, to attenuate a source of unhappiness. Yet it is the drink that ultimately prolongs their suffering. The very same principle was at work for Abd-ar-Rahman. It turned his pursuit of fame, wealth, and pleasure into a vicious cycle.

Consider fame. In 2009, researchers from the University of Rochester conducted a study tracking the progress of 147 recent graduates in achieving their goals.[22] Some of the alumni had previously described "intrinsic" goals, such as developing deep, enduring relationships. Others had "extrinsic" goals, such as achieving a good reputation or fame.

The results brought good and bad news. The good news: By and large, the subjects did achieve their stated goals. They basically got what they had aimed at. But be careful what you wish for, because only the alumni whose goals were intrinsic had happier lives. Those whose goals involved wealth and image found unhappiness instead. The people who attained their extrinsic goals experienced more negative emotions, such as shame and anger. They even suffered more physical maladies such as headaches, stomachaches, and loss of energy.

This is one of life's cruelest ironies. The unhappiest people I have ever met are those most dedicated to their own self-aggrandizement—the pundits, the TV loud-mouths, the media know-it-alls. They build themselves up and promote their images but feel awful most of the time.

Talk about the paradox of fame. Just like drugs and alcohol, once you become addicted, you can't live without it. But you can't live with it, either. Celebrities report that fame brings "severe loss of privacy" and "a deep loss of trust," according to research by the psychologist Donna Rockwell.[23] Yet they can't give it up.

But it's not only celebrities who are at risk. The impulse to fame by everyday people has generated some astonishing innovations. One is reality television, in which ordinary folks convert their day-to-day lives into performances for others to watch. Why? "To be noticed, to be wanted, to be loved, to walk into a place and have others care about what you're doing, even what you had for lunch that day: that's what people want, in my opinion." Those are the words of one twenty-six-year-old participant in the early hit reality show *Big Brother*.

Then there's social media. Today, each of us can build a personal little fan base, thanks to Facebook, YouTube, Twitter, and the like. We can broadcast the details of our lives to friends and strangers in an astonishingly efficient way. That's good for staying in touch with friends, but it also puts a minor form of fame-seeking within each person's reach. And the evidence confirms the anecdotes: This can be a source of unhappiness.

It makes sense. When is the last time you saw someone post honest negativity on Facebook? "My boss just chewed me out for being lazy!" "My wife doesn't find me attractive since I went bald!" "My kid is failing math! #brutal." No, everyone posts smiling selfies of their hiking trip with friends. They build a fake life, or at least an incomplete one, and share it.

As a result, the rest of us consume almost exclusively the incomplete lives of our media "friends"—and then compare their illusions to our reality. It's a funny exercise, when you think about it: We spend part of our time pretending to be happier than we are, and the other part of our time seeing how much happier others seem to be than we feel.

Pride can be a powerful toxin. So can another canonical hedonistic pleasure: lust. From Hollywood to college campuses, the growing assumption among "enlightened" people is that sex is inherently liberating, and sexual variety is normal and good.

This assumption actually has a name. We can call it the "Coolidge Effect"—and yes, it is named after the thirtieth president of the United States. The story (probably apocryphal) begins with Silent Cal and Mrs. Coolidge touring a poultry farm. The first lady, surprised that there were very few roosters, asked how so many eggs could be fertilized. The farmer informed her that the virile roosters did their jobs over and over again every day. "Perhaps you could point that out to Mr. Coolidge," she supposedly joked.

The president, hearing the remark, followed with a query of his own. He asked whether the rooster serviced the same hen each time. Oh, no, the farmer told him. There were many hens for each rooster. "Perhaps you could point that out to Mrs. Coolidge," said the president.

Perhaps those were happy roosters. But does the same principle work for us, as modern culture is fond of suggesting?

It does not. This isn't my moral opinion; it's what empirical evidence tells us. In 2004, two economists decided to analyze whether sexual variety led to greater well-being. They examined data from about 16,000 adult Americans, asking their subjects (confidentially) how many sex partners they had had in the preceding year and how happy they felt.[24] Across men and women alike, the resulting data meant the researchers could discern the optimal number of partners if happiness was the goal.

The answer: 1. (Abd-ar-Rahman had about 5,999 too many.)

If egotistical and physical gratification are both traps, what about riches and luxuries?

We already learned that money only buys happiness up to a point. Remember, additional income raises the happiness of the poor quite quickly. Escaping poverty and joining the middle class solves a whole host of problems.

But above the level of subsistence, it takes enormous increases in income for even small amounts of happiness. The renowned psychologist Daniel Kahneman has carefully chronicled how marginal dollars hardly buy any happiness after approximately $75,000 (for a family of four).[25] Moving from middle class to rich will not solve whatever problems you have left.

Think about it. Almost by definition, all you're left with at that point are the problems money can't crack. Your wife or husband won't like you more when you move from $75,000 to $125,000. Your kids won't suddenly stay out of trouble. You won't have a better relationship with God.

Furthermore, the new things that you can buy will probably ultimately prove unsatisfying. A close friend who had risen to great wealth as an entrepreneur explained this to me. Needless to say, I was more than a little skeptical. "You *really* want me to believe that I couldn't buy awesome stuff if I had a billion dollars?" I asked. He replied with a story.

When he was beavering away to start his firm, with hardly anything in the bank, he made a promise to keep himself going: "When I finally make it, the first thing I'm going to do is buy a Mercedes. In cash!" Well, one day, he realized he had made it. He could do just that. So he drove down to the dealership. And what did he find out? "The Mercedes was a nice car, for sure. But it really wasn't much better than my old Toyota."

Even when people get wealthy, they almost never feel like they are "there." This is a reflection of a very human phenomenon called the "hedonic treadmill," where our expectations speed up almost seamlessly to match our resources. People are naturally acquisitive. Research on this phenomenon shows that no matter how much people earn, they tend to say they need about 40 percent more to have "sufficient" income. The day after you start making $100,000, you'll feel convinced you really need $140,000.[26]

Another one of Kahneman's findings is even more interesting than the $75,000 threshold. He finds that our belief that we *should* be happier continues to rise with more money, even after the actual happiness levels off. We define success using a social script that tells us more money is always better, and we cling to this script even when it has completely ceased to describe our actual emotional experience. That big raise won't bring you much extra happiness, but you will intellectually feel that you *ought* to be happier—after all, you're doing better by society's standards!

So for most of the readers of this book, more money really won't buy happiness. And worse yet, just because money has little impact on happiness, that doesn't mean it cannot provoke unhappiness—remember, happiness and unhappiness aren't just opposites. When we obsess over money as an end in itself, we all know it can generate misery.

Nobody has described the snares of materialism more famously than St. Paul in his First Letter to Timothy: "For the love of money is the root of all evil: which while some coveted after, they have erred from the faith, and pierced themselves through with many sorrows." If you like your proverbs pithier, try the Dalai Lama: As he likes to say, it is better to *want what you have* than to *have what you want*.


All this might seem vaguely paradoxical. After all, we are unam-biguously driven to accumulate material goods, to seek fame, to look for pleasure. It's in our nature to seek these things. How can it be that these very things can give us unhappiness instead of happiness?

In short, our evolutionary cables have crossed. We assume that things we are attracted to will relieve our suffering and raise our happiness. My instincts tell me, "Get rich and famous." They also tell me that unhappiness is lousy. So I conflate the two, presuming that getting rich and famous will make me less unhappy.

But herein lies Mother Nature's cruel hoax. She doesn't really care whether you are unhappy or not. She just wants you to want to pass on your genetic material. If you conflate intergenerational survival with your personal well-being, that's your problem, buddy, not hers. This is only exacerbated by nature's useful idiots in society, who propagate a popular piece of life-ruining advice:

"If it feels good, do it." Unless you share the same life goals as bacteria and protozoa, this is a really bad rule of thumb.

We chase after these worldly goods to reduce our dissatisfaction, and find only more dissatisfaction in the process. We sense that nothing has full flavor. We crave something more, but we can't quite pin down what it is that we seek. Without a great deal of reflection and spiritual hard work, doubling down on ego and eros can seem like the best paths available.

But these things don't fill the inner emptiness. They may bring brief satisfaction, but it never lasts and is never enough. And so we crave more.

This paradox has a word in Sanskrit: *upādāna*, which refers to a cycle of craving and grasping. Here is how the Dhammapada (the Buddha's Path of Wisdom) explains it: "The craving of one given to heedless living grows like a creeper. Like the monkey seeking fruits in the forest, he leaps from life to life." Further, "Whoever is overcome by this wretched and sticky craving," the text explains, "his sorrows grow like grass after the rains."

The thirst for admiration, the hunger for material things, and the habit of objectifying others—this very cycle of grasping and craving—follows a formula of the world that is elegant, simple, and deadly:

*Love things and use people.*

This was Abd-ar-Rahman's formula as he sleepwalked through life. It is the snake oil peddled by the culture makers from Hollywood to Madison Avenue. But we know in our hearts that it is morally disordered and a road to misery. We want to be free of the sticky cravings. We want to find a formula that actually reduces unhappiness.

How about this:

*Love people and use things.*

By simply inverting the deadly formula, we render it virtuous. I offer this to you as a creed for the pursuit of happiness. Of course, this is easier said than done. It requires the courage to repudiate pride and the strength to love others—family, friends, colleagues, acquaintances, God, even strangers and enemies. Only deny love to things that actually are *things*. Few things are as liberating as giving away to others that which we hold dear. And few things produce greater unhappiness than materialism.

How does all this square with every American conservative's belief in the free enterprise system? A critic of capitalism might well point out that all the mistakes I have been enumerating—pursuing money, pleasure, and fame—are facilitated by free enterprise. Is our precious economic system just a shortcut to misery?

One of my favorite jokes captures this critique perfectly.

An American businessman is visiting a small Mexican fishing village. He notices a small boat tied up at the dock. He's surprised to see the boat idle, since it is about 1 p.m.—prime fishing time. The businessman walks over to investigate, peers into the boat, and spies one happy fisherman and one large tuna. He compliments the fisherman on his catch and asks how long it took to nab it. The Mexican man replies that it only took an hour.

"Well, why didn't you stay out longer to catch more?"

The fisherman replies that he has enough to fulfill all his immediate needs.

"So what do you do during the rest of the day?"

"I sleep late, take a nap, drink a little wine, and play guitar with my friends, señor."

At this, the American is appalled. "It's your lucky day—I'm a Harvard MBA. Let me give you some advice. First, you have got to spend more time fishing and save the money. Pretty soon, you'll be able to buy a bigger boat and hire a few men to work for you. After a while, you can buy several boats and hire more crews. Eventually, you'll have a whole fleet, and so you can sell your catch

directly to the processor. Maybe even open your own cannery."
Now he's really picking up steam. "At that point, you could leave
this small coastal village and move to Mexico City—maybe even
Los Angeles! You could run your whole business from there."

The fisherman ponders all this for a minute. Then he asks,
"How long will all this take?"

"I'd say about twenty or thirty years."

"But what then, señor?"

"What then?! You can sell your whole enterprise for a fortune!"

"A fortune? Wow! Then what?"

The American has to think for a moment. Then it comes to him.
"Then," he triumphantly declares, "you can retire and do whatever you want! For example, you could move to a quaint, beautiful
fishing village where you could sleep late, take a nap, drink wine,
and make music with friends!"

Now, this joke might seem suited to the critics of capitalism,
not to a conservative like me. This misses the point. We can measure the value of our lives in whatever currency we choose. Some
prioritize great success in the workplace; others prefer an early
retirement and the chance to pursue hobbies. Free enterprise empowers us to make that choice for ourselves.

No, the real moral of this joke is an ends-means distinction.
Material things must never be sought for their own sake; we must
recognize them as means to achieve greater, nobler things. Materialism is tyranny, and no ideology or economic system is immune
to it. Anyone who has spent time in a socialist country must concede that selfishness and rent-seeking behavior are at least as bad
under socialism as when markets are free.

It is true, though, that free enterprise puts material prosperity
within the reach of more people than ever before. It universal-
izes trade, exchange, and the goal of upward mobility. In a way, it
might make materialism easier to attain, just as being a pharmacist makes it easier to get narcotics than if you are a plumber.

So does that mean free enterprise presents a problem for our formula for happiness? Does it lead us into the trap of *un*happiness?

These questions demand an answer, and I looked all over the world for it. And that's how I found myself in New Delhi.

## ABUNDANCE WITHOUT ATTACHMENT

The Swaminarayan Akshardham Hindu temple in New Delhi, India, is one of the most amazing things I've ever seen. Consecrated in 2005, it took 7,000 artisans working full-time to carve all the gods, goddesses, people, and animals out of sheer rock. It sits on one hundred acres. And it was where I made friends with a penniless Hindu swami named Gnanmuni.

Swami Gnanmuni (pronounced "Gyon-moony") is the administrator of the temple. We had never met before, but I'd caught wind of his reputation. If Yelp reviewed monks, he would have had five stars. A man in his late forties, the swami is a monk following absolute vows of chastity and poverty. He has utterly renounced the material world.

I'm not sure what I was expecting, but it certainly wasn't flawless English. Yet as I approached, that's exactly what I heard. And what was that accent—Texas?

"How ya doin'?" The swami's greeting was avuncular. Within two minutes, he'd referred to me as "dude."

Gnanmuni's journey, I soon learned, could give my own nontraditional life a run for the money. He grew up in Houston, the son of an Indian engineer. He excelled in school and enrolled at the University of Texas at the age of sixteen. (He joked that his orange robe was evidence of his Texas Longhorn spirit.) After completing a bachelor's and three master's degrees, including an MBA, he went to work as a management consultant. The money came quickly.

But, like so many of us, Gnanmuni never felt fully satisfied with the material world. As he walked through the temple with me, he described his sense that a more transcendental, less materialistic life had been beckoning to him. At twenty-six, he wasn't ready to concede that this was all there was.

It was then that Gnanmuni had his awakening. He gave up his business career, renounced his possessions, traveled to India, and enrolled in a Hindu seminary. Six years later, he emerged a monk. From that moment on, the sum total of his worldly possessions has been two robes, some prayer beads, and a wooden bowl. He is prohibited from even touching money.

What would this rebel who had left the capitalist world behind have to say about free enterprise? I took a deep breath, and posed my query nonetheless: "Swami, is free enterprise good or bad for the soul?"

His response was rapid. "It's a good thing! It has saved millions of people in my country from starvation." This was not quite what I expected. "But you own almost nothing," I pressed. "I was sure you'd say that money is corrupting."

He laughed at my naïveté. "There is nothing wrong with money, dude. The problem in life is *attachment* to money."

The formula for the best life, as he told it, was this:

*Abundance without attachment.*


Some might be scratching their heads over Swami Gnanmuni's enthusiastic endorsement of the first part—abundance. It turns out that this is an utterly uncontroversial assertion, even in traditions commonly perceived as ascetic.

Don't believe it? Then let's go meet none other than His Holiness the Dalai Lama.

In 2013, I trekked to the Himalayan foothills with two of my AEI colleagues to visit the Dalai Lama at his base in Dharamsala, India. His Holiness has lived there since being driven from his Tibetan homeland by the Chinese government in 1959. He is to this day one of the most revered religious leaders in the world—respected by Buddhists and non-Buddhists alike, and totally dedicated to human happiness.

Very early one morning during the visit, I was invited to meditate with his monks. About an hour had passed when hunger pangs began, but I worked hard to ignore them. It seemed to me that such earthly concerns had no place in the superconscious atmosphere of the monastery. Incorrect. Not a minute later, a basket of freshly baked bread made its way down the silent line, followed by a jar of peanut butter with a single knife. We ate breakfast in silence, and resumed our meditation. This, I soon learned, is the Dalai Lama in a nutshell: transcendence and pragmatism together. Higher consciousness and utter practicality rolled into one.

Later, over tea we spoke with His Holiness about the need to make the pursuit of happiness the ultimate goal of public policy. The title of one of my books—*Gross National Happiness*—actually came from the neighboring Buddhist kingdom of Bhutan, where the king had established the happiness of his people as the measure by which the success of his country should be judged. I told His Holiness that AEI's mission was to harness the power of free enterprise to make it possible for more people to pursue their happiness. Would he be willing to visit us and spend a few days to discuss his concerns about capitalism with American conservatives in a spirit of love and openness? He readily agreed, and joined us for a public summit at AEI's headquarters in February 2014.

The result was magic. At first, his visit caused confusion. Some people couldn't imagine why he would visit us; as *Vanity Fair* magazine asked in a headline, "Why Was the Dalai Lama Hanging Out with the Right-Wing American Enterprise Institute?"

There was no dissonance, though. When asked why he came to AEI, the Dalai Lama explained, "I felt, rightist also human being. . . . Their main purpose is how to build happy society."

During our discussions, he returned over and over to two practical yet transcendent points. First, his secret to human flourishing is the development of every individual. In his own words: "Where does a happy world start? From government? No. From United Nations? No. From individual."

Further, like Swami Gnanmuni, the Dalai Lama has no hostility to abundance. In fact, Tibetan Buddhists actually count wealth among the four factors in a happy life, along with worldly satisfaction, spirituality, and enlightenment. Money per se is not evil. Indeed, unprecedented abundance means that more and more people can access more and more of the material things they need. This is why any moral system that takes poverty relief seriously has to celebrate the ahistoric economic bounty that has been harvested these past few centuries.

The real issue, the Dalai Lama explains, is not wealth per se, but rather our delusion that "satisfaction can arise from gratifying the senses alone." Another word for this delusion: *attachment*. Sound familiar?

In Tibetan, the English word *attachment* is translated as *do chag*, which literally means "sticky desire." It signifies a desperate grasping at something, motivated by fear of separation from the object. One can find such attachment in many dysfunctional corners of life, from jealous relationships to paranoia about reputation, professional standing, and material possessions.

When we become excessively attached to wealth, when we forget that material prosperity and worldly pleasure are not virtuous ends in themselves, we do ourselves and our world a disservice. And lest you think that this is all purely Eastern philosophy, you can find the same ideas almost by dropping the needle any-place in the Bible. For example, "Whoever loves money never has enough; whoever loves wealth is never satisfied with their income. This too is meaningless." That's not Tibetan Buddhism; it's Ecclesiastes 5:10.

What's so bad about attachment? In the realm of material things, it results in envy and avarice. Sidestepping these pitfalls is critical to life satisfaction. The formula for a happy, meaningful life is to appreciate abundance while avoiding attachment.

I took the Dalai Lama's—and Swami Gnanmuni's and St. Paul's and Ecclesiastes's—advice to heart. But how do we put that into practice? Moreover, how do we apply those lessons to a real-world philosophy?

To learn that, I had to dive back into the research. What I found were three strategies, three best practices for avoiding attachment while enjoying abundance.

### 1. Collect experiences, not things.

Material things appear to be permanent, while experiences seem evanescent and likely to be forgotten. Early on in our marriage, when we had next to no money, Ester and I had a dilemma. We had just enough money to go on a short vacation, or we could buy a couch. Not both. Ester argued that a weekend away would be better. I argued that the couch was something we'd have forever.

We compromised—and took the vacation. But in retrospect, Ester was right. Twenty years later, when we look back, we still remember the weekend away in great detail. If we had bought the couch instead, it would be gone and forgotten. Though it defies conventional wisdom, it is physically permanent stuff that evaporates from our minds. It is memories in the ether of our consciousness that last a lifetime, there for us to enjoy again and again.

This "paradox of things" has been thoroughly documented by researchers. In 2003, psychologists studied how Americans remembered different kinds of past purchases—both material things and experiences.[27] They found that reflecting on experiential purchases left their subjects significantly happier than did remembering the material acquisitions.

But more than any study, I learned this lesson once and for all from one of my sons. Six years ago, when Carlos was only nine, he announced that all he wanted for Christmas was a hunting and fishing trip for the two of us. No toys; no new objects at all. Just the trip. Just us.

So we went hunting and fishing. And we have gone every year since. Any toy we could have bought him would have been broken or collecting dust by now. Yet both of us can tell you every place we've gone together and every critter we've bagged—every single year.

## 2. Avoid excessive usefulness.

Our daily lives often consist of a dogged pursuit of practicality. We want everything around us to be *useful*. But this is a sure path toward the attachment we need to avoid. Aristotle makes this point in his *Nicomachean Ethics*, a theory of happiness that still towers over most other philosophy 2,300 years after it was written. Aristotle shows admiration for learned men because "they knew things that are remarkable, admirable, difficult, and divine, but useless."

Doing things for their own sake—as opposed to instrumentalizing every moment in pursuit of distant goals—makes for mindfulness and joy. As Vietnamese Buddhist monk Thich Nhat Hanh describes it, "While washing the dishes one should only be washing the dishes, which means that while washing the dishes one should be completely aware of the fact that one is washing the dishes."[28]

That's an abstract way to drive home a very practical point. Countless studies back up that wisdom. In one famous experiment, college students were given puzzles to solve.[29] Some of the students were paid, but others were not. It was the unpaid participants who tended to continue to work on the puzzles after the formal experiment was finished. By contrast, the paid participants abandoned the task as soon as the session was over. The fixation on rewards vacuumed all the pleasure out of the task. And sure enough, the paid subjects reported enjoying the whole experience less—even including the payout!

What makes you happier: a meeting with colleagues or a game of cards with friends? The answer is the activity you pursue for the sheer joy of it. Unless you're one of the rare people with a passion for meetings, the things you look forward to are probably those that lead to no other gain than enjoyment itself. A night at the movies with your family, riding a bike, going to a ball game, having dinner with someone you love. These are terrible investments in purely financial terms. They are all "useless" in a purely economic sense. But they are precisely the sorts of things that Aristotle and a Buddhist monk knew would bring us happiness.

This does not mean we should abandon productive impulses. I am not calling for the end of industrialization and a universal call to artisanal basket-weaving. What I am calling for is a world in which we all treat our industry as an intrinsic end in itself.

### 3. Get to the center of the wheel.

In the rose windows of many medieval churches, one finds the famous *rota fortunae*—the "wheel of fortune." The concept is borrowed by Christianity from ancient Romans' worship of the pagan goddess Fortuna. Following the wheel's rim around, one sees the cycle of victory and defeat that everyone experiences throughout the struggles of life. At the top of the circle is a king; at the bottom, the same man as a pauper.

Chaucer's *Canterbury Tales* uses the idea to describe important people brought low throughout history: "And thus does Fortune's wheel turn treacherously. And out of happiness bring men to sorrow."

The lesson went beyond the rich and famous. Everyone was supposed to remember that each of us is turning on the wheel. One day, we're at the top of our game. But from time to time, we find ourselves laid low in health, wealth, and reputation.

If the lesson ended there, it would be pretty depressing. Every victory seems an exercise in futility, because soon enough we will be back at the bottom. But as the Catholic theologian Robert Barron writes, the early church answered this existential puzzle by placing Jesus at the center of the wheel.[30] Worldly things occupy the wheel's rim. These objects of attachment spin ceaselessly and mercilessly. Fixed at the center was the focal point of faith, the lodestar for transcending health, wealth, power, pleasure, and fame. The least practical thing in life turned out to be the most important and enduring.

There is an important lesson for us embedded in this ancient theology. Namely, woe be unto those who live and die by the slings and arrows of worldly attachment. To prioritize these things is to cling to the rim, a sure recipe for existential vertigo. Instead, make sure you know what is the transcendental truth at the center of your wheel, and make that your focus. Move beyond attachment by collecting experiences, avoid excessive usefulness, and get to the center of your wheel.


By the way, I never finished my story about Swami Gnanmuni. Before I left him that day in Delhi, we had a light lunch of soup and bread. I told him I would be recounting our conversation in my book and that many Americans would be hearing his name.

He contemplated this for a moment and, modeling nonattachment, responded simply.

"Dude, do you like the soup? It's spicy."

## THE PURSUIT OF HAPPINESS

So there you have it, a few simple lessons for happy warriors with a conservative heart, dedicated to the pursuit of happiness—their own, and that of others.

First, we should concentrate each day on the happiness portfolio: *faith, family, community,* and *earned success through work.* Teach it to those around you, and fight against the barriers to these things.

Second, resist the worldly formula of misery, which is to use people and love things. Instead, remember your core values and live by the true formula: *Love people and use things.*

Third, celebrate the free enterprise system, which creates abundance for the most people—especially the poor. But always remember that the love of money is the root of all evil, and that the ideal life requires *abundance without attachment.*

The rest of this book is dedicated to applying these three lessons in politics, policy, and, most important, ordinary life. Armed with this knowledge, we turn first to the people who most need a hand up in their pursuit of happiness: the poor.

# Chapter 2

# WHY AMERICA HASN'T WON THE WAR ON POVERTY:

## Spending Trillions Without Moving the Needle Where It Matters Most

For most of our nation's history, the key ingredients for happiness were common knowledge throughout America. No matter how much money they made or how educated they were, the vast majority of citizens were united in a civic culture that prized the institutions of faith, family, community, and work.[1]

My AEI colleague Charles Murray shows in his bestselling book *Coming Apart* that this is no longer the case.[2] Tragically, the secrets to a flourishing life have become less of a universal birthright and more of a luxury good. More and more, these building blocks of the pursuit of happiness are disappearing in the communities that need them most of all.

Today, the poorest 20 percent of American adults are only a fifth as likely to be married as the richest 20 percent. They are about 30 percent more likely to say they never attend religious services and over 60 percent more likely to say they never spend time with neighbors.[3] They also work, on average, about 20 percent fewer hours per week. These patterns are decidedly not concentrated in any racial or ethnic group. As Murray shows in great detail, they afflict all sorts of economically vulnerable Americans.

In other words, modern American poverty goes far beyond financial need, as though that weren't bad enough. Of course, many low-income Americans do enjoy great lives filled with faith, family, community, and work. But on average, poor communities are disproportionately deprived of these four secrets to happiness. Combine all this with the added strain of material deprivation, and it comes as no surprise that Americans in the bottom fifth are only half as likely to say they are "very happy" about life as are those in the top fifth (18 to 36 percent).

We could argue endlessly about causality. Do work and family dysfunction cause poverty, or vice versa? Probably both. But whichever way the cycle runs, the effects on happiness are undeniable. If conservatives want to rebuild the pursuit of happiness for everyone, we need to start with poor Americans. We need to understand both the cultural factors and the economic circumstances faced by America's most vulnerable citizens. We must grasp why poor communities in America have stagnated while poverty has plummeted around the world, and why our sprawling entitlement programs have mostly failed to improve poor people's lives. And we have to start explaining how conservative solutions can solve the problem.

This will require a major update of conventional conservative "up-by-your-bootstraps" mythology. I cannot count the number of frustrated elected officials who have explained to me how the aspirational, rags-to-riches stories they've been telling their whole career just don't connect with voters anymore. It turns out there's a reason for that. To be sure, conservatives should never cease to emphasize personal responsibility and hard work. But we must also acknowledge that failing schools and stagnant wages have made simple effort an insufficient guarantee of thriving in large swaths of America.

This new approach will also require an autopsy on decades of failed progressive policies. Government technocrats have spent trillions of dollars standing up sprawling bureaucracies that have succeeded only in making poverty marginally less painful. They have failed to make it less permanent.

To do these things, we have to look squarely at the ugly truth about poverty in America today.

## ROSA LEE'S STORY

In September 1994, a *Washington Post* reporter was exposing Americans to a shocking, slow-motion tragedy.[4] The journalist, Leon Dash, had spent three years following and speaking with a woman named Rosa Lee Cunningham. The stories he collected became an eight-part, 39,000-word masterpiece that took the newspaper a week to publish. It won prestigious awards, including a Pulitzer Prize.

When I first read the series, I could scarcely believe it. For me and many other Americans, it permanently changed the conversation about poverty.

Born in 1936, Rosa Lee was raised in Washington, D.C. Life was difficult from the beginning, and she underachieved in school.[5] She became a mother at fourteen and had seven more kids, fathered by five different men. Her only marriage began at age sixteen and lasted less than a year: An abusive husband turned out to be even worse than the abusive mother she was trying to escape.

Life did not improve for Rosa Lee after the federal government's massive antipoverty programs began in the 1960s. Her material needs declined marginally, but her misery continued unabated. She was a lifelong shoplifter and, at different times, a prostitute, a heroin dealer, and eventually a heroin user. Rosa Lee went to jail a dozen times throughout her adult life. She was complicit in the crime and drug addiction of six of her children. Desperate for money, she prostituted her own daughter at age eleven. And at the age of fifty-eight, she died of AIDS, unsure if she contracted it through sex or by sharing needles.

Dash painted the squalid truth of modern poverty in stark colors. His story shocked readers so much that the *Post* had to set up a special hotline for fans and critics of this one series. Two decades later, reading the story is still like staring at a car accident. You can't stand it. But you can't turn away.

It is scarcely believable that anything like this could happen in modern America. Yet it did. Even more disturbing, such extraordinarily tragic stories were unfolding in neighborhoods just a few blocks from the White House, decades *after* a War on Poverty had been declared by the president of the United States. Dash shines a spotlight on this irony in one particular anecdote: As Rosa Lee weeps for her daughter who has been arrested for murder, a television in the background is tuned to Bill Clinton's inauguration. She ignores it. Rosa Lee has never voted: "It's not going to make one difference in my life."[6]

Still, government was not absent from Rosa Lee's life. To the contrary, all throughout the story, the government is a focal point. It appears in the form of a revolving-door criminal justice system, and as a major player in the miserable ecosystem that aided and abetted her destructive behavior.

In every chapter of her story, some well-intentioned government program rears its head in a perverse way. On the first of the month, when welfare checks are cashed at the corner liquor store, they are used for drugs as well as rent. Family members and drug dealers demand payments and loans taken from her government support check. Public housing is used as a safe haven for crime. People exaggerate their roles in caring for children to elicit additional aid and food stamps.

In short, in Rosa Lee's story, the welfare system is a nameless, faceless wellspring of poorly directed resources. She feels entitled to the assistance and is utterly dependent upon it, but it fails to fundamentally change her tragic life.

Except perhaps to make her life worse. A man who fathered three of her children wanted to join Rosa Lee in a stable family. But he never did. Dash asked why. "Back in them days," Rosa Lee explained, "the welfare didn't permit no man to live with you. That's how I lost him. We were going to try to live together, but the welfare wouldn't let us."[7] The man had a job, but Rosa Lee didn't see how they could make it without welfare.

Not all of Rosa Lee Cunningham's family was a disaster. Two of her sons formed stable families and held solid jobs. These sons had two key victories in common. With the encouragement of dedicated male mentors, both resisted drugs and earned their own livings. Their seemingly random success amid all the chaos was hard for Dash to understand:

> *How is it, I wondered, that many . . . had prospered against considerable odds while some, like Rosa Lee, had become mired in lives marked by persistent poverty, drug abuse, petty and violent crime and periodic imprisonment?*[8]

The series did not meet with universal praise. Some readers denounced the reporting as racist because Rosa Lee Cunningham was African American. (So was the reporter.) The *Post* received more than 4,600 calls in response to the series, and many were blistering. But most callers praised the story.[9] Readers recognized that Rosa Lee's story was being repeated in communities of all ethnicities. They understood that the entire country was implicated in this disaster.

At its core, Rosa Lee's case was a story of institutionalized human degradation. In her impoverished youth, she suffered the scandal of pre-1960s poverty. As an adult, she was caught in a dystopian government system that allowed the worst behavior to thrive and tended only to the most glaring material needs of the poor through cold, hard cash. Government myopically managed to this one metric—money—while society forgot about the human beings like Rosa Lee whose lives were at stake.

## THE FAILURE OF THE WAR ON POVERTY

How did our nation fail Rosa Lee Cunningham, even as we invested trillions of dollars specifically to help her and the rest of America's poor?

To answer this question, we need to travel back to May 22, 1964. It was on that day, in Ann Arbor, Michigan, that President Lyndon B. Johnson formally announced the Great Society. A few months earlier, Johnson had declared an "unconditional war on poverty" in his State of the Union address.[10] But at Ann Arbor, the president explained that his vision was about much more than simply eradicating poverty:

*The Great Society rests on abundance and liberty for all. It demands an end to poverty and racial injustice, to which we are totally committed in our time. But that is just the beginning. The Great Society is a place where every child can find knowledge to enrich his mind and to enlarge his talents . . .*

*where men are more concerned with the quality of their goals than the quantity of their goods. . . .*

*[It is] beckoning us toward a destiny where the meaning of our lives matches the marvelous products of our labor.*[11]

What was the ultimate goal of the Great Society? Johnson put it clearly: ". . . to pursue the happiness of our people. Our success in that pursuit is the test of our success as a Nation."

That encompasses much more than the alleviation of material need. Johnson was pledging to bring true human flourishing within every American's reach. He pledged that every one of our citizens, whatever their origins, would have the chance to expand their talents, earn their success, and pursue happiness.

These are wonderful and noble goals. They are worthy of a great nation. Have we met them?

The day before Johnson delivered that speech, I was born in Spokane, Washington. I am, quite literally, a child of the Great Society era. That means that both the Great Society and I just turned fifty, which is a good time to pause and reflect. Johnson laid out a clear test to measure "our success as a Nation" in his effort. So, is government successfully pursuing "the happiness of our people"?

There has been at least one undisputed victory. The Great Society's crusade for civil rights culminated in the Civil Rights Act, the Voting Rights Act, and other overdue steps that ended legal discrimination in our country. Today, African Americans still face many barriers to their pursuit of happiness, but Jim Crow laws are not one of them. This is a tremendous achievement of the American people.

But what is the Great Society's legacy on poverty? That question is much more complicated.

Let's start with poverty understood most narrowly—pure material need. The situation was dire as Johnson stepped up to the

podium. Just a few months prior, in January 1964, *Life* magazine
had published a photo essay titled "The Valley of Poverty." Shocking images detailed the plight of people living in eastern Ken-
tucky's Appalachian Mountains.

> *Their homes are shacks without plumbing or sanitation. Their*
> *landscape is a man-made desolation of corrugated hills and*
> *hollows laced with polluted streams. The people, themselves—*
> *often disease-ridden and unschooled—are without jobs and*
> *even without hope.*[12]

One photo showed a family eating a dinner of surplus com-
modities in a room wallpapered with sheets of newspaper. Another showed a man and his son scavenging for frozen lumps of
coal to heat their overcrowded home. The lives on display shocked
the nation.

In addition to this crushing rural poverty, need also gripped
America's cities. In 1964, nearly half of the 34 million Americans below the poverty line lived in large cities and bleak sub-
urbs.[13] Most poor families in the 1960s lacked a car. Most lived
in cramped quarters without a bed for each family member. Unbelievably, while most of the poor were white, fully *half* of all non-
white families fell below the poverty line.[14]

What has happened in the ensuing decades? Fortunately,
day-to-day life below the poverty line has become much less un-
comfortable. Both the length and quality of life have increased
dramatically among the poor, infant mortality has fallen, and
access to public education has expanded.

In 2011, the average poor American possessed more living
space than the U.S. average for all citizens in 1980.[15] And that's
even more living space than the average person today across *all*
economic classes in France, Sweden, Germany, and the United

Kingdom. Three-quarters of poor Americans today have one or more cars.[16] Most have refrigerators, dishwashers, televisions, and microwave ovens. Enjoyable items like personal computers, video game consoles, and Internet access have become commonplace.[17]

To give an idea how these things have become within reach of the poor, take a quick example. In 1964, a color television cost $379. That is about $2,849 in today's dollars,[18] meaning it was an unimaginable extravagance for most Americans. When I was a kid, a color TV was totally out of the question for a lower-middle-class family like mine—we had a black-and-white Zenith that you had to whack every half hour when the picture conked out. Today, a forty-inch flat-screen TV costs $220 at BestBuy,[19] placing it within the reach of most Americans.

Most of the lifestyle improvements listed above are due to technological progress. But some of the reduction in material deprivation can indeed be attributed to Great Society programs. To the extent that government played a role in increasing the availability of food, medical care, and housing, we should celebrate. But we have to consider an important caveat before we declare the Great Society any sort of success: Poverty was already in retreat when Johnson turned on the government spigots.

In 1950, roughly 25 percent of Americans were officially poor.[20] By 1966, just two short years after the War on Poverty formally began, the number was down to 14.7 percent. That 10 percent drop translates into a 41 percent cut in the poverty rate—a truly amazing accomplishment. Surely, you might be thinking, Johnson's government-centered agenda was a stunning success!

There's just one problem with that narrative. Almost all of the decrease in poverty took place *before* Johnson's policies went into effect. It was a vibrant economy that did the trick.

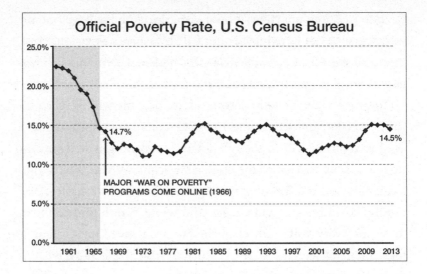

In the 1950s, the U.S. economy grew by a remarkable 4.25 percent per year, on average.[21] Growth was even stronger in the 1960s, averaging 4.53 percent.[22] Many economists (me included) believe that much of this prosperity flowed from President John F. Kennedy's supply-side tax cuts, which reduced rates across the board by 20 percent. For some perspective, consider that our growth in the 1950s and '60s was *two-and-a-half times* the anemic percent growth rates we've averaged over the last decade. Suffice it to say things were going well.

As a result of this economic expansion, the poverty rate had already fallen from 25 percent in 1950 to 19.5 percent by the morning Lyndon Johnson strode to the podium in 1964. By 1966, as major Great Society efforts like Medicare were struggling to get off the ground,[23] the poverty rate had fallen further to 14.7 percent. Like some especially image-savvy general, LBJ publicly declared war on an enemy that was in the middle of beating a hasty retreat. Thanks mainly to free enterprise, America was already winning the War on Poverty by the time Johnson's initiatives were up and running.

In other words, what happened in America in the 1950s and '60s is exactly what happened abroad after 1970. Free enterprise wiped out a massive amount of poverty. But this reduction was arrested soon after the War on Poverty began. The poverty rate in 1966—when a few of President Johnson's programs had been implemented and many others were still coming on line—was 14.7 percent. In 2013, at least $15 trillion later, the poverty rate in the United States of America had fallen all the way to . . . 14.5 percent.[24]

By any fair standard, the government's War on Poverty would be classified as a failure. Certainly, any private-sector CEO would be fired under remotely equivalent circumstances.

Now, many policy experts (on both left and right) complain that the poverty rate is a flawed metric. They argue that the official measure of poverty is a poor way to measure people's material standard of living. That's because the official metric actually excludes many of the most prominent government transfer programs that aim to reduce deprivation. What's more, it doesn't take into account other important phenomena, such as (as we just saw) the falling price of many modern conveniences.

This argument is true as far as it goes. But just because it doesn't count food stamps or cheap televisions, the official poverty rate is not useless. That's because, in addition to some government assistance, it does capture most of the total resources that families *earn for themselves*. If the trillions we've spent on the Great Society had helped huge numbers of Americans become self-sufficient and empowered them to earn their own success since the mid-1960s, we would see a big drop in the official poverty rate.

Yet no such drop took place. Since the first day that all the major policy pillars of the Great Society were in place, the poverty rate has dropped only by 0.2 percent. That is basically a rounding error. Instead of boosting poor Americans into the workforce and on a trajectory toward the middle class, government programs have only helped them subsist in poverty by attending to a few physical needs.

In 1951, just 3.8 percent of Americans received some sort of public aid; that's about one out of every 25 people.[25] By 2012, it was 32.3 percent. And while uptake of government help was increasing roughly ninefold, fewer and fewer Americans were working. The percentage of men in the workforce—either working or seeking work—has dropped from 81 percent in 1964 to just 62.7 percent today. We can also calculate the percentage of noninstitutionalized men aged 20–64 who are not working: That figure increased from 6 percent to 17 percent. Of all the working-age men who are neither in prison nor in the military, one in six are now idle.

So here is the true story of American poverty over the past five decades: fewer paychecks, more welfare checks, and no meaningful increase in earned success. Trillions in government spending have not bought us more hope or more opportunity—only a little less material misery.

This is precisely what LBJ promised the Great Society would *not* accomplish. Three months after his speech, as Johnson signed his Economic Opportunity Act in the Rose Garden, he declared:

> *We are not content to accept the endless growth of relief rolls or welfare rolls. We want to offer the forgotten fifth of our people opportunity and not doles. Our American answer to poverty is not to make the poor more secure in their poverty but to reach down and to help them lift themselves out of the ruts of poverty and move with the large majority along the high road of hope and prosperity.*[26]

If all we sought to do was make government assistance and material goods more available to people living in poverty, we've performed quite well. America's free enterprise economy, with an assist from a few effective government initiatives, has made poverty marginally more tolerable. And again, this is not to be taken lightly. Reducing true indigence is a triumph. Erasing the very worst aspects of material deprivation is an accomplishment our society should take pride in.

But our true goal was nowhere near that materialistic or narrow. Our ultimate objective, as President Johnson stated, was much loftier. America set out to arm every citizen with the opportunity to build a meaningful life that stirs their passions and engages their talents. We never agreed to settle for a little less suffering. We were aiming at the pursuit of happiness well understood. That meant helping people achieve a dignified life.

But instead of providing struggling people with an escape rope out of poverty, the War on Poverty simply made that unsatisfying condition more bearable. Instead of growing opportunity, it grew the welfare rolls.

The fact that we have hardly moved the needle on earned success after spending trillions of dollars is not merely a failure of public policy. It is the greatest moral scandal of our time.

## POVERTY ISN'T COMPLICATED—IT'S COMPLEX

What system could produce such unacceptable results? Were the architects of the War on Poverty diabolical fanatics intent on creating socialism and servitude? Was it all some grand scheme to create a permanent underclass, wholly reliant on government, that would always vote a certain way?

Of course not. There is not a shred of evidence that LBJ and his team were not genuinely trying to relieve poverty. American prosperity was surging in the wake of World War II, yet millions from inner-city Chicago to the Mississippi Delta were trapped in abject poverty. The president wanted to act. Most of us would have, too.

And while the approach Johnson chose was deeply flawed, it's not like his ideas faced real competition from the right. Conservatives were unhappy with the War on Poverty because they correctly saw where it was headed, but they offered no credible alternatives. The strategy of the political right in the 1950s and '60s was to stand "athwart history, yelling 'Stop' " (to use William F. Buckley Jr.'s famous phrase). But when it came to fighting poverty, "Stop!" was a losing proposition—as well it should have been.

"Stop" something that might rescue the most destitute people in Appalachia from hunger and malnutrition? "Stop" something that might help a poor grandchild of slaves rise from poverty and pursue his or her happiness? Conservatives had no moral standing to oppose Johnson's War on Poverty, because they had no vision of their own to help these people.

They also, as it happens, had no power. Democrats held the Senate (67–33), the House of Representatives (256–177), and the White House. Johnson was on his way to dismantling Republican Barry Goldwater in the November 1964 election (61 percent to 39 percent). At the federal level, America was essentially a one-party state. A new progressive era was at hand. But as we know, that yielded a War on Poverty that generated little "progress" at all.

LBJ's intentions were certainly good, and the goals he envisioned were noble ones. The fatal problem was his methods. They were rooted in profound misunderstanding about what government could and could not do. The failure of Johnson's policies to achieve his stated ends stemmed from a failure to recognize a crucial distinction: the difference between *complicated* problems and *complex* problems.

*Complicated* problems are extremely difficult to understand, but they can be resolved with sufficient money and brainpower. And once you find the solution, the problem is permanently solved. You can replicate the solution over and over with a high degree of success. Designing a jet engine is a complicated prob-

lem. Figuring out how to build the first jet engine took sophis-
ticated tools, computing ability, and expert engineers. But once
engineers figured out how to do it—and designed a jet engine that
worked—they could replicate the process and make jet engines
routinely.

*Complex* problems are very different. They initially seem simpler to understand but can actually never be "solved" once and for
all. One example is a football game. You know exactly what success looks like—it's when your team wins. (In my case, it's when
the Seattle Seahawks win.) But there are so many trillions of com-
binations of things that can happen on the playing field, so many
variables and ambiguities, that even the best data and strategies
are dwarfed by the uncertainty that remains.

Here is a simple example of how complicated and complex
problems are confused. Before the 2015 Super Bowl, CBS News
ran a story titled "Prediction Machine Picks Seahawks over Patriots in Super Bowl XLIX."[27] It reported on a website called
"PredictionMachine.com," which "uses some of the most ad-
vanced analytics available today and analyzes them through a
machine they call 'the Predictalator,' which is 'the most in-depth,
state-of-the-art sports prediction software ever created.'" The
Predictalator crunched all the data—everything from strength of
regular season schedule, to injuries, each team's record against the
same opponents, and individual player stats. And it determined
that "if the Super Bowl were played 50,000 times, the Seattle Seahawks would come out on top 57.3 percent of the time." Unfortunately for me, that was not the case in the actual Super Bowl,
which the Seahawks got to play only once that year. They lost,
28–24, in soul-crushing fashion.

The fact that the football game is complex and not complicated
is, in fact, why millions of people love watching the game. We
have no real idea what is going to happen. Great teams can begin
a game almost certain to win and end up losing.

If designing a jet engine were a complex problem, you'd fall out of the sky most of the time. If a football game were a complicated problem, you'd know the score before it started just by looking at the team rosters.

This difference is the fundamental reason why the War on Poverty failed. Its architects thought poverty in America was more like a jet engine than a football game. They maintained the conceit that with their big brains and a boatload of taxpayer money, they could smoothly categorize all the facets of poverty and design mechanistic programs to "solve" them.

This delusion is the central thread that links iconic progressive policies from those of Woodrow Wilson to FDR, LBJ, and all the way to the present day, with proposals from free community college to "Cash for Clunkers." Anyone who relies on government solutions to fundamentally complex social problems thinks that America is one big *complicated* problem, fixable through the scientific method.

This is what the economist Friedrich Hayek termed "scientism." It's the conceit that human problems can be solved like a system of equations—as if people were as predictable as the laws of physics. This was the idea behind nineteenth- and twentieth-century theories like Friedrich Engels's "scientific socialism" and Woodrow Wilson's "scientific public administration." The former killed tens of millions of innocents; the latter exploded the size of the federal government.

Poverty is a dynamic human phenomenon that varies with incentives, imperfect information, and the behavior of the people. This is what central planners' pride prevents them from seeing. Their boundless optimism in the pseudoscientific state is simply a practical and philosophical error—think of it like fantasy football, but with human lives at stake. The federal government is spending almost $1 trillion a year on eighty different antipoverty programs without moving the poverty rate because bureaucrats don't get *real* football.

This is not to suggest that fighting poverty is a futile endeavor, any more than it is futile for the Seahawks to take the field on Sundays. While there is no one mathematical formula for winning a football game, there are winning teams and losing teams. What separates them? Three things above all: work, culture, and values. And no surprise, these are precisely the elements of success in all complex human endeavors, from business to family life. When we apply those principles to the fight against poverty, we won't "solve" the problem of poverty—but we can win more often than not, and make real progress in alleviating suffering and need.

And this is not just conjecture. In fact, for a brief time in our history, we made real progress, doing just that.

## THE END OF WELFARE AS WE KNEW IT—OR SO IT SEEMED

By the time Leon Dash was chronicling the life of Rosa Lee Cunningham in 1994, Americans were fed up. It had become clear that the War on Poverty had fomented a culture of dependency. That culture was expensive, sure. But more important, it was hurting the people it was intended to help.

Americans might have been willing to waste money indefinitely, but they were not willing to destroy their fellow citizens' lives, especially the most vulnerable. There was an appetite for change. And it was at this moment that we enjoyed a rare bright spot in the War on Poverty. It was called *welfare reform*.

Awareness of the need for reform had been growing for a long time. I remember as a kid hearing people refer to their welfare checks as their "salary." Even at a young age, I knew the difference between a salary and a welfare check, and my family saw what confusing the two could do to others. Whether or not they had read exposés like the *Washington Post*'s, everyone knew the system was bad news.

After a protracted political battle against the Democratic Party's left wing, Congress finally passed a series of reforms in 1996. Among other things, the changes imposed time limits on how long people could receive welfare support and required that people work to receive benefits.

This was not some right-wing counterattack on the welfare state. To be sure, the germ of welfare reform started with conservatives. Some were scholars at think tanks like AEI. Others were practitioners, like Wisconsin governor Tommy Thompson, who proved that reform could help people move toward independence. But at the national level, it took collaboration between Republican legislators and a Democratic president to make reform a reality. Everyone had to risk his or her political capital in order to fight for people and the pursuit of happiness.

When Bill Clinton finally signed the Personal Responsibility and Work Opportunity Reconciliation Act of 1996 in the Rose Garden, he invited a special guest to join him. She was Lillie Harden, a forty-two-year-old mother from Little Rock.

Ten years earlier, Clinton had invited Harden to speak at a meeting of governors and share her experiences making the leap from welfare to work. Clinton remembered how, in front of forty-two other governors, he had asked her what the best thing was about being self-sufficient. "When my boy goes to school," she told Clinton, "and they say what does your mama do for a living, he can give an answer."[28]

"I have never forgotten that," Clinton said as he signed welfare reform into law. "From now on, our nation's answer to this great social challenge will no longer be a never-ending cycle of welfare. It will be the dignity, the power, and the ethic of work."

And welfare reform rooted in conservative principles proved to be a success. You don't even have to take a conservative's word for it. Here is President Clinton, describing the outcomes on the tenth anniversary of the reforms:

> *In the past decade, welfare rolls have dropped substantially, from 12.2 million in 1996 to 4.5 million today. At the same time, caseloads declined by 54 percent. Sixty percent of mothers who left welfare found work, far surpassing predictions of experts. . . . More than 20,000 businesses hired 1.1 million former welfare recipients . . . child poverty dropped to 16.2 percent in 2000, the lowest rate since 1979, and in 2000, the percentage of Americans on welfare reached its lowest level in four decades.*[29]

In the three decades before reform, the number of Americans on welfare had never significantly decreased. A single decade after reform, the number had fallen by more than half. Millions of poor Americans were finally experiencing the promise of the Great Society. These supposedly unemployable people were beginning to earn their own success.

As work increased, so did happiness. One study found that the self-reported happiness of single mothers improved substantially due to welfare reform.[30] The changes to this system help explain why the "happiness gap" between single mothers and the rest of the population shrank significantly from 1972 to 2008.[31]

It was a great moment for our country. Pragmatic conservative reformers had partnered with a flexible liberal president to stanch the bleeding from ineffective antipoverty policy. And contained in this victory were two important lessons.

First, government can help the poor when it recognizes that poverty is a *complicated* problem and not a *complex* one. The safety net is not hopeless by definition. It does not always turn people into government-dependent drones. Welfare reform showed that the system could be salvaged by requiring work and limiting the duration of benefits, except for those who truly could not work. Government must work with human nature instead of trying to override it.

Second, it was clear that the right kind of reform could meaningfully improve the quality of life for many of the country's most vulnerable. Those who made the transition from welfare to work did not merely achieve a reduction in their material poverty. They took a dramatic step toward the holistic human flourishing that the country's leaders had promised when they launched the Great Society. They were, in Johnson's words, finally moving "with the large majority along the high road of hope and prosperity."

Welfare was becoming what it was always meant to be—temporary help, not a permanent condition. And this is still what Americans want it to be. In 2009, the year Barack Obama took office, one poll asked whether Americans agreed with the statement, "Able-bodied adults that receive cash, food, housing, and medical assistance should be required to work or prepare for work as a condition of receiving those government benefits." That view was supported by 92 percent of liberals and 97 percent of conservatives, by 96 percent of Democrats and 97 percent of Republicans.[32] In a polarized age when right and left agree on little, such consensus is remarkable.

Optimists assumed that welfare reform was permanent and that the principles of work-based safety net programs would migrate to other programs for the poor. The 1996 changes focused primarily on one program, Aid to Families with Dependent Children (AFDC), which was renamed Temporary Assistance for Needy Families (TANF). That program reached just 4.2 percent of American households in 1983, and just 2 percent by 2011. Clearly this is only a small corner of the massive web of programs that provide food, housing, and cash assistance to the poor.

Surely the success of welfare reform would inspire politicians to apply the same lessons in other areas. Right?

Wrong. Instead of spreading work-based reform, it was stopped through a reactionary backlash, led by those who never made peace with welfare reform in the first place. Scientific public administration reared its head once again.

## WELFARE AND POVERTY TODAY

It happened in 2008: the perfect storm for public policy. America entered its worst economic recession in seventy years. Housing prices fell approximately 30 percent.[33] For millions of Americans whose wealth was tied to their homes, this amounted to a collective loss of $6 trillion.[34] The stock market, as measured by the S&P 500 index, fell by 57 percent.[35] And the net worth of all U.S. households declined by $16 trillion—a 24 percent drop.[36] Almost nine million Americans lost their jobs.[37] Six years later, the U.S. economy had still not returned to full, prerecession employment.

Amid these economic nightmares came the election of President Barack Obama, who had the aim of implementing traditional progressive policies through a newly energized federal government. With the House and Senate also in Democratic hands, Obama could make good on his word. He passed a massive economic stimulus spending bill, encouraged a Federal Reserve that added unprecedented amounts to the money supply, regulated the financial system in broad new ways, and brought huge parts of the health-care system under a new degree of government control.

Welfare spending also massively increased under the Obama administration. From 2009 to 2013, welfare spending totaled $3.7 trillion, according to one Senate report.[38] That is almost five times what the federal government spent on transportation, education, and NASA combined over that period. And all the while, the administration was attempting to undo the bipartisan work requirements of welfare reform. Since the 1996 law was passed and signed, the states had been required to have at least half of their adult welfare recipients in qualified "work activities." But in 2012, the U.S. Department of Health and Human Services asserted for itself the brand-new authority to issue waivers to this requirement whenever it saw fit.

More important than anything else, though, the administration was turning its attention away from poverty per se and instead toward the old progressive bogeyman of income inequality. Indeed, the president spoke less about the poor than his predecessors. A 2013 analysis by one researcher at Georgetown University found that President Obama mentioned the poor less than any president in decades.[39] In his public statements and official communications on social class, he mentioned the poor only a quarter of the time he mentioned a social class; in contrast, Ronald Reagan talked about the poor in two-thirds of his public pronouncements.

Instead, the conversation was turned toward the income gap between rich and poor Americans. The president declared income inequality a "defining challenge of our time"[40] that "undermines the very essence of America."[41]

Like any great narrative, the administration's inequality story had villains: wealthy people and conservative Americans. In an extraordinary series of attacks, Mr. Obama repeatedly accused ordinary citizens who disagreed with his ideology of not caring about the people his own economic policies had left behind.[42] He called Republicans' ideas "thinly veiled social Darwinism," painting their goals as "pulling up those ladders [of opportunity] for the next generation."

With comments like these, the president was not just disagreeing with conservatives; he was saying we are morally bankrupt. We don't care about people who are out of work. We don't care about people born into poverty. We don't care about people in need.

Conservatives across the country were indignant at their president's ad hominem attacks. But armed with neither a substantive antipoverty agenda of their own nor the moral language to accurately attack the administration's failure, they lacked a productive outlet for their frustration.

It is bad enough that in the face of absolute deprivation, the focus would be on relative poverty in the form of inequality. But it is the height of irony—and evidence of catastrophic government ineffectiveness—that inequality actually *increased* over the course of the Obama administration. In fact, the rich have gotten richer and the poor have gotten poorer.

Consider the facts. The top half of the economy has, in fact, recovered from the Great Recession in fine style. Since January 2009, the Dow Jones Industrial Average has more than doubled in value. The year 2013 brought the largest annual increase in the S&P 500 since the late 1990s. And the rewards of this sustained market surge were mostly reaped by a select few.

According to New York University economist Edward Wolff, the top 10 percent of American earners now own 81 percent of stocks and mutual funds, 95 percent of financial securities, 92 percent of business equity, and 80 percent of nonhome real estate.[43] As a result, economic growth that is ginned up through investment markets (by, say, creating money) will prove to be extremely regressive. And sure enough, a whopping 95 percent of the real income growth from the economic recovery flowed directly to the much-regretted "1 percent."[44] (Skeptics may note that this last finding belongs to Emmanuel Saez, a left-leaning economist who collaborates with famous French economist Thomas Piketty.)

During the recovery, Americans in the top 5 percent (with average incomes of more than $320,000) were the only group of U.S. households to see their average inflation-adjusted incomes rise between 2009 and 2013. All other income groups experienced a decline in real income over that period.

And how about the bottom 20 percent of U.S. households? That group of earners was hit the hardest during the recovery. Their real incomes fell by 7 percent on average from 2009 to 2013, the largest percentage decline of any group.[45]

Predictably, dependence on the government by the poor has increased massively. The number of Americans receiving food stamps has increased dramatically.[46] Today, one in seven Americans are so poor that they require food assistance to bring home enough for their children to eat.

At the same time, the number of people on government disability insurance has surged by 20 percent. This is not because of an unprecedented epidemic in workplace accidents, but rather because disability effectively serves as permanent unemployment for millions of desperate Americans. These Americans are not getting rich. The average monthly benefit was $1,165 in 2015, or an annual income of about $14,000.[47] People are so desperate today that many have given up on finding work and are willing to live in what amounts to permanent poverty-level subsistence.

While the tide of dependence for the poor has crept forward, work has receded. As we have already noted, the labor participation rate, which measures how many citizens are working or seeking work, fell to 62.7 percent in October 2014. That's the smallest fraction since the days of the Carter administration. Millions have given up hope of ever finding work again, and have dropped out of the labor force entirely, which has the perverse effect of appearing to lower the official unemployment rate. A sarcastic tweet from one *New York Times* reporter put it perfectly: "We are basically 'recovering from the recession' by reducing the share of Americans who participate in the labor force. Hurrah!"

According to an analysis by the Associated Press, the unemployment rate for the top 20 percent of the income distribution in America (those earning $150,000 or more) was 3.2 percent in 2013, three years after the end of the recession. Statistically, that is considered full employment. For the bottom 20 percent (those earning less than $20,000) the unemployment rate was over 21 percent.[48] The average unemployment rate for African American teenagers has risen to 33.2 percent.[49] And none of these figures includes people who have given up looking for work and dropped out of the workforce. Only those who are actively looking for jobs but can't find them are counted as "unemployed."

To put all this in perspective, in 1932—the very worst point of the Great Depression—the national unemployment rate was 22.9 percent.[50] So for those in the bottom of the economy today, the employment rates of the Great Depression are virtually indistinguishable from those of our economic "recovery."

And what has happened to income inequality? A central theme in each of the president's campaigns, this is one metric by which a committed egalitarian progressive might judge this administration. Economists calculate income inequality with a measurement called the "Gini coefficient"—a number from 0 to 1, where zero denotes perfect equality, and 1 would be complete inequality (think of only one household with 100 percent of all income). Since January 2009, the Gini coefficient for U.S. household income has moved from less than 0.47 in 2009 to 0.48 in 2013. That's right, income inequality is getting worse.

The facts are clear. We have a robust and growing economy for high-income Americans. But for those at the bottom, the opportunity to work, rise, and earn success is disappearing. The administration's ostensibly pro-poor, tough-on-the-wealthy agenda has led us toward a new American Gilded Age. We are increasingly becoming two Americas. In one America, there is practically unlimited opportunity and prosperity. In the other America, where those at the bottom reside, we are still in the depths of the Great Depression.

Instead of real solutions and genuine hope, those stuck at the bottom today have been offered class resentment and presidential sloganeering about the evils of rich people and political conservatives.

## WE NEED A BETTER SOLUTION

Let's review. After five decades and immense sums of money, our government seems content with making poverty a little less insufferable. Today, yet another White House is promising different results using the same old policy tools. And the poor are falling further behind.

Given these results, why does America keep returning to this stale, ineffective playbook? It's not as though voters are crazy. Rather, it's that everyone knows we must do *something* to help struggling people, and the old ideas appear to be the only ones on offer.

Conservatives have been quick to criticize the welfare state, and those critiques are often justified. But importantly, our alternatives have generally been almost nonexistent. This is not even close to sufficient. It's little wonder that Americans actually believe it when President Obama claims conservatives don't care about the little guy. One typical survey, conducted in September 2013 by the *Huffington Post* and YouGov, found that 51 percent of

Americans thought the GOP was most interested in helping the rich. Twenty-eight percent said the middle class. Only 7 percent said the poor.[51] In October 2010, the Democrats held an 11-point lead over Republicans as the party "more concerned with needs of people like me." By October 2014, that lead had nearly doubled to 21 points (54 to 33 percent).[52]

It's hard to convince people to give you the reins of power when more than half think you don't care about them. And more specifically, it's impossible to convince them you can revamp the welfare state when only fewer than one in ten think you will put poor people's interests first.

Five simple facts capture the sorry state of affairs we find ourselves in today:

1. Our nation is leaving the vulnerable behind, and Americans rightly find this unacceptable.

2. The War on Poverty has not been successful, and the last seven years have made things dramatically worse.

3. Americans know these facts and are instinctively skeptical of conventional large-government welfare policies.

4. While conservatives have criticized those outmoded policies, they have offered little in the way of alternatives.

5. Americans have concluded this is because conservatives don't really care about the poor.

A half century of conventional wisdom has failed in the fight against poverty. The materialistic, mechanistic view of human development that a big-government approach presumes makes holistic solutions impossible. The only way to set things right is for conservatives to show we care and offer a new vision for the country. This new vision must be guided by the optimism of opportunity. It must declare peace on a prudent, reliable safety net for those who truly need it. It must harness the tools of private entrepreneurship, acknowledge the profound value of hard work, and echo the moral clarity of the Good Samaritan.

Where can we find such a vision? Not in a university classroom. Not even in a think tank. We can find it, it turns out, from men who used to live on the street.

# Chapter 3

# PUSHING THE BUCKET:

## How Honest Work Ennobles
## and Elevates Us

Dallas Davis grew up with an absent father, an alcoholic mother, and no role models. By the seventh grade, he dropped out of school. At the age of fifteen, he had already left home and joined a gang. His life revolved around drugs and alcohol—and doing whatever it took to acquire them.

To a young teenager with few options, this lifestyle probably once looked like a glamorous escape. But it was soon unmasked as a deadly trap. Dallas ended up living on the streets of New York. During the freezing cold winters, he sought refuge in churches, in abandoned buildings, and eventually in Grand Central Terminal. It was there, under the grime-covered constellation of stars that decorate the station's ceiling, that Dallas accidentally discovered the path to a better life.

One especially frigid day, Dallas lay huddled under a blanket in a corner of the terminal when a strange man walked up to him. He introduced himself as George McDonald, a name that was already familiar among the Grand Central homeless. A gruff, working-class Catholic, George had spent hundreds of nights handing out sandwiches to the people who called the terminal home. Local regulations didn't exactly smile upon this pastime: Feeding the homeless had gotten George arrested four times.

Dallas was stunned by the gesture. "I had already just about given up on life," he explained later.[1] "I was dirty, stinking, nasty and disgusted with myself." But when George spoke to him, "[w]hat I saw in his eyes was not just kindness or compassion, but *recognition*. He recognized that I was a human being." George extended a simple courtesy to homeless men and women that hardly anyone else did. He treated them like real people.

That was a lot. But it wasn't enough, as George learned from another homeless person, a woman known simply as "Mama." On Christmas Eve in 1985, when he was distributing presents along with the usual meals, George presented Mama with a gift-wrapped scarf and wished her a Merry Christmas.[2]

It was the last time George would see her alive.

When the terminal closed around 1:30 a.m., the transit police forced the homeless out into the sub-twenty-degree night. Mama curled up next to a subway grate and waited out the hours until the terminal reopened. She made her way back inside and lay her weary body down on a wooden bench in the main waiting room. A few hours later, as children across the city leapt out of warm beds and tore into their presents, a police officer found Mama on that bench.[3]

She had died—a nameless "Jane Doe" for the city—still clutching the scarf George had given her.

When George heard about Mama's death, the news pierced his heart. Handing out sandwiches and small gifts was great as far as it went, but it didn't go far enough. People needed a sandwich to get from today to tomorrow. They needed *dignity* to build a real future. And that meant they needed not just to accept charity, but to give their own efforts and be valued for them.

And so, after much thought and discussion, George and his wife, Harriet, went big: They started a homeless shelter and job training organization for men called the "Doe Fund" in Mama's honor. Homeless men—many coming straight from prison—would live in a converted Harlem schoolhouse; learn to work and earn; stay clean and sober; and graduate, ready to enter society as value-creating, values-conscious individuals. The Doe Fund's objective was not merely to help homeless people survive from day to day. It was to empower them to reclaim their lives through the dignity of real, valuable, honest-to-goodness work.

The Doe Fund was up and running the next time Dallas Davis met George McDonald, in 2009.

Dallas did not come straight from Grand Central, however. Like many other men enmeshed in taking and selling drugs, he had gone to prison. Now he was about to be released, and he realized he had nowhere to go. His family wanted nothing to do with him, and his old associates would send him spiraling right back into old habits.

That's when Dallas saw a prison flyer advertising the Doe Fund's "Ready, Willing & Able" program. He remembered his encounter in Grand Central Terminal and the dignity with which George had treated him. And so, when he got out of prison, Dallas begged his counselor for a referral. She arranged an interview at the Doe Fund's Harlem Center for Opportunity.

Even to a program that specialized in hard cases, Dallas's record looked rough. He had been kicked out of previous shelters and programs after getting into fights and returning to drugs. As a result, Nazerine Griffin, the director of the Harlem Center, was looking skeptically at the ex-con who sat across from him in a shirt and tie.

But "Naz," as he is known, wasn't just a Doe employee. He was also an alumnus. A drug dealer who had become his own best customer, just a few years earlier Naz had found himself lying facedown on the pavement, hiding from police beneath a parked car. He made his way into a drug treatment program, but had no place to go upon completion except one of the city's homeless shelters. It was a depressing place that, in his words, "warehoused human beings," with no way out.

In a search for better options, he found his way to the Doe Fund, and was an early graduate in 1998. Eleven years later, his job was screening applicants for this very program.

Naz is tough, as Dallas soon learned. "Are you ready to change your life?" he asked forcefully. "Are you truly willing to put the work in?"

Dallas told Naz he was ready. But even in these hard questions, he detected something different from what he had experienced before in his life. "I had been through so many institutions in my life—jails, group homes, drug programs. They always told me what they could do for me. But this was the first time I was told what I could do for myself."

Naz took him at his word, and admitted Dallas, giving him his shot at a fresh start. After orientation, Dallas was assigned to "push the bucket" as one of the Doe Fund's "Men in Blue." This was and still is the first rung of the ladder for new entrants. Each day, Doe Fund trainees don bright blue uniforms, grab brooms and buckets, and clean 150 miles of New York City streets and sidewalks.

Dallas initially hated the idea of such work. But lo and behold, "It turned out I didn't mind it at all. In fact, I kind of liked it."

That might sound implausible, but anyone who has ever found moments of peace in an ordinary task can relate. Pushing the bucket gave Dallas time to think. It gave him the chance to form concrete goals he could meet and exceed. It gave him a reason to set his alarm every morning. "Before long," Dallas says, "I started realizing I wasn't just picking up trash from the streets. I was picking up values, morals, and principles. I was picking up self-esteem. And then when I would look back at the block I had just cleaned, and would see what a great job I had done, I realized that I had picked up pride."

Over the next few months, Dallas did all the big routes. He pushed the bucket in Harlem River Park, in East Midtown, on Madison Avenue and even Park Avenue. He became a familiar face to commuters. "I remember seeing well-dressed people on their way to work . . . walk by me and say, 'Hi, Dallas!' These well-dressed people on Park Avenue—speaking to me!"

When he was homeless, people would avert their eyes and pass Dallas as quickly as possible. Now the commuters on his Park Avenue route said hello, and some even knew his name. Of course, it should embarrass New Yorkers that it took a blue uniform for Dallas to be treated with a shred of respect. But Dallas was thrilled.

That winter, New York was hit by a huge snowstorm that paralyzed the city. While most were huddled in their homes, Dallas and his fellow Men in Blue ventured out into the frozen city. They swapped their brooms for shovels and started clearing the streets. Dallas could not believe how far he had come. "We were out there making paths for the elderly, for the children, for people to get to work. Here we were, people who had slept in the garbage, in train stations, under bridges—those who society once thought couldn't accomplish anything. We were the ones bringing the city back to life."

Those big moments started piling up. He had always put on a macho façade, but as he held the first paycheck of his entire life in his hands, Dallas began to cry. The Doe Fund pays more than the minimum wage, but the amount on the check was not what moved Dallas to tears. It was what the check represented. "Someone really believed I could do something—and that it was worth paying me to do it." That had never happened to him before.

After three months of pushing the bucket, Dallas was unstoppable. He enrolled in one of the Doe Fund's skilled jobs programs that taught energy-efficient-building maintenance. That meant waking up daily at 4:30 a.m. to study before breakfast. He learned how to fix boilers and sprinklers, received certification from the Occupational Safety and Health Administration, and finished at the top of his class. Just imagine how that felt to a guy who had dropped out of middle school and spent twenty years thinking he had zero value and zero future.

Dallas was even chosen to address his fellow graduates as the Doe Fund's commencement speaker. "My name is Dallas Davis," he began. "And I am proud to say that I am standing here before you tonight with a full-time job and my own place to live, with my finances in order, with a renewed relationship with my children." The place went wild.

Looking back, Dallas says that Ready, Willing & Able did for him "what my teachers couldn't do, and what those judges and program directors couldn't do, [and that] is show me that I have potential. . . . That is what George McDonald must have seen in my eyes all those years ago in Grand Central Terminal."

Dallas Davis's story is remarkable. But even more remarkably, it is not unique. Since 1990, the Doe Fund has helped more than 22,000 people reclaim their lives. Its success is amazing when you consider that most of its trainees are drug-addicted, homeless felons—many previously incarcerated for violent crimes. These are the hardest of the hard cases. These are the people who many, deep down, do not see as capable of taking part in the American Dream. They are the ones whom polite society has given up on, and who have given up on themselves. But the Doe Fund has found a way to help them reassemble the shards of their lives into new, meaningful, and dignified adventures.

How do they do it? How does the Doe Fund succeed where so many have failed? I needed to go to New York and find out for myself.

Walking through the doors of the former schoolhouse that is now the Doe Fund's Harlem Center for Opportunity is like stepping into an oasis of hope. Outside is one of New York's toughest, bleakest neighborhoods. But inside there are signs of edification and encouragement everywhere you look.

One of the first things you see when you enter is a sign that reads, "Work is love made visible." The cafeteria, where formerly homeless people train for restaurant work, features the words of Dr. Martin Luther King Jr.: "All labor that uplifts humanity has dignity and importance and should be undertaken with painstaking excellence." From Naz's office to the dishwashing area, that principle is on display everywhere.

When George and Harriet took over the old school, they refurbished the dilapidated building. In came a wood-paneled library, classrooms with computers, a recreation room with a big-screen TV, and a beautiful patio that overlooks the Harlem River. These furnishings contradicted some advice from on high. "The city and government officials said, 'You don't want to make them too nice because they won't want to leave,'" George told me, amused. "Of course, that's from a person who has not slept in a room with nine other men." But George insisted on facilities that offered a physical manifestation of the Doe Fund's core principle: serious, genuine investment in every man who comes through its doors.

I had come to the Doe Fund because George and Harriet invited me to give a lecture for the trainees. I was all set to discuss some of my latest research exploring the factors that make for a happy life. But five minutes talking with the Men in Blue made me want to throw away my notes. These men didn't need any PhD lectures from a skinny think tank president with hipster glasses. I needed to learn from them.

And the more I listened, the more I kept thinking: It's not just me. *America* needs to hear this. These principles and practices are how this country can repair its broken approach to poverty. As the last chapter made clear, our society—through conventional welfare policies—has been all too willing to write off some subset of our neighbors, seeing them as burdens to be managed at minimal expense. We must reject this, and proclaim that all people are moral equals. The men and women of the Doe Fund understand this, because they have experienced it in their own lives. They have more to teach us about the conservative heart than any government study ever could.

I promised my new friends I would share what they taught me. So here are four key lessons that animate the work of the Doe Fund. These are the lessons that I believe should animate the conservative heart to build a new way of helping the poor in a country that has increasingly left them behind.

## LESSON 1. PEOPLE ARE ASSETS, NOT LIABILITIES.

When you walk by a homeless man, what do you see?

George and Harriet have a clear answer. They genuinely do not regard a man living on the street as a liability. Instead, they have the mindset of optimistic entrepreneurs. They see an underutilized asset.

In the business world, how do you handle a liability? First, you try to get rid of it. If you can't, you manage it, minimizing the problems it causes and the costs it imposes. That is exactly what many cities do with homeless men and women. Though they are staffed by an army of well-meaning people, the flawed system crams people into shelters filled with plenty of drugs and vermin but precious little hope. People subsist, mostly, but they rarely have the chance to flourish.

But when George and Harriet come across men sleeping in the park, they see precious human resources. They see what an innovative Peruvian economist named Hernando de Soto calls "dead capital"—dormant assets with deep intrinsic value that simply need to be enlivened.

This is most definitely *not* a materialistic point, that people are just potential moneymaking machines. On the contrary, to see people as assets to society means that they can create value denominated however you wish—which is what it means to be made in God's image.

Understanding this, George and Harriet became social entrepreneurs. They aimed to bring all this human capital back to life. And they work toward this by reminding every man of his inherent capacity to work, to serve others, and to become a productive part of the community. In short, they identify the value the current system overlooks and find a way to activate it.

This project faces mighty odds, which is why most people have given up on these men, and indeed why they have given up on themselves. Seventy percent of Doe Fund enrollees have been convicted of a crime. Most have abused drugs or alcohol.[4]

Studies clearly show that people with these characteristics do very poorly, on average. According to the Justice Department, of the 700,000 people released from state and federal prisons each year, two-thirds of state prisoners and 40 percent of federal prisoners are rearrested or have their supervision revoked *within three years*.[5] Six in ten former inmates are unemployed one year after release.[6]

Doe Fund graduates demolish these statistics. Six months after moving on to full-time work, seven in ten Ready, Willing & Able graduates have retained their new positions. An evaluation commissioned by the New York State Division of Criminal Justice Services and conducted by Bruce Western of Harvard University found that Doe Fund graduates are 60 percent less likely to commit a felony in the three years after completing the program than their peers released into the shelter system.[7]

These remarkable data flow from one simple principle. George, Harriet, and their colleagues see the potential for real happiness in every single person they meet. They see that potential in addicts and dealers. They see it in criminals and convicts. They see it in the homeless and the hopeless. And their work is to get these men to *pursue* that happiness through the earned success that comes from honest, hard work.

When people walk through the door of the Harlem Center for Opportunity, it is the first time that many of them have ever been treated like a valuable asset. And when you treat people with dignity and respect, a funny thing happens: They respond by earning that trust.

Economics are just a small part of this, but the data are well worth looking at. Since its founding, the Doe Fund's social enterprises have generated more than $750 million in revenue. That's nearly a billion dollars in "dead capital" brought to life by a bunch of homeless men because one couple saw them as assets to empower and not liabilities to manage. About a third of all that revenue has gone straight into the pockets—more accurately, the brand-new savings accounts—of the Men in Blue. That is money they have used to reconstruct lives of independence and self-sufficiency. And by helping homeless men become productive citizens, the Doe Fund estimates it has saved New York an additional $3 billion in social costs.

Think what it would mean if these results were scaled up to

the rest of America. At this writing, the U.S. labor participation rate—the percentage of the population that is either working or looking for work—is the lowest it has been since the 1970s.[8] Millions of Americans have simply given up trying to find jobs and have dropped out of the labor market entirely. Moreover, in June 2014, some 7.5 million Americans were stuck in part-time jobs they didn't want because they could not find full-time work. That's up from just 4.4 million in 2007.[9]

We can debate who's to blame for this tragedy. But put that aside for a moment. Think instead of the breathtaking opportunity at our fingertips. If 22,000 homeless men can produce $750 million in revenue through work, and find purpose in life at the same time, imagine what this whole country could accomplish.

## LESSON 2. WORK IS A BLESSING, NOT A PUNISHMENT.

When you pass the homeless man on the street, maybe you give him a dollar or even buy him a sandwich. People debate whether these acts are good or bad. My wife—who has made our car into a rolling food pantry for people begging at intersections—once gave a homeless man a whole pie (apple I think).

But even if you give generously, nobody seriously suggests that this is what homeless people truly want. It is crazy to imagine a homeless man who is satisfied with his lot. Every human being aspires to earn his own success.

George McDonald learned this firsthand as he was distributing sandwiches. "They said over and over again they appreciated the sandwich—but what they really wanted was a room and a job to pay for it. And I heard that enough that I was convinced that they wanted to work."

But there was an obvious problem. Few homeless and formerly

incarcerated men can grab the first rung of the economic ladder, and many fewer manage to climb it. They have no education and no work experience, a rap sheet that makes them even less appealing than others with equally empty résumés. They have virtually no chance of finding a job.

That's why the nucleus of the Doe Fund's approach is paid, transitional work. That all begins, as we learned, with "pushing the bucket." It's easy to imagine some people bristling at this part of the program. Isn't it disrespectful to take vulnerable people and pay them to make Park Avenue prettier for shoppers and commuters?

But this perspective assumes something important. It assumes that paying work is only dignified once it reaches a certain threshold of prestige. Being a college professor or an engineer is dignified work, to be sure. But sweeping streets or flipping burgers? These are terrible punishments that capitalism unfairly inflicts on people! Somewhere in between white-collar careers and "dead-end jobs" there is an imaginary line where dignity kicks in. Beneath that line, better not to work at all.

This assumption is widespread in America today. It also happens to be dead wrong. The real truth, which George and Harriet have found, is both simpler and more subversive: Work with reward is always and everywhere a blessing.

Does that mean we should ignore social mobility? Turn a blind eye to the complex factors that can keep people from climbing the economic ladder? Of course not. But as we consider these challenges, our thinking must start with the truth that work is vastly better than no work for the soul. Honest, productive work per se is never a punishment. Work is a blessing.

Of course, this doesn't mean that much coming from me alone. Like many lower-middle-class Americans, I did my share of low-skilled work, and it taught me a lot about real life. But nobody is pretending that this compares to the struggles of millions of adults who cannot grab steady hold of meaningful jobs.

So don't take my word on this subject. Take it from the people who know—people like Devon Greene, another graduate of Ready, Willing & Able.

Devon Greene had a tough start in life. His mother died of AIDS when he was six years old. His grandmother did her best to provide for him, but she did it by allowing dealers to sell drugs from inside her home. Several more moves later, Devon was arrested and confined to the Youth Block at New York City's Rikers Island prison. It's a place, he says, where the guards are just as dangerous as the gangs.

But the chaos brought clarity. "It was there, in the middle of all the violence and chaos, that I knew I had to make a choice. Was this going to be my life? Or was I, Devon, going to do something about it? I chose to change." And just like Dallas Davis, Devon soon found himself pushing the bucket.

And like Dallas, Devon wasn't pushing it for long. "The harder you work, the more opportunity comes your way. One success turned into another and then another. And if you take those opportunities as they come, and work as hard as you can, there's no stopping them, no stopping you."

Today, there really is no stopping Devon. He is twenty-three and in his first year of college, earning his bachelor's on full scholarship. He has a job at Mount Sinai Hospital, where he was recently named "employee of the month." He isn't picking up trash anymore, but he still feels like he's pushing the bucket—away from his old life, and toward a bright future.

Richard "Rick" Norat, another remarkable man, fought back tears as he explained how pushing the bucket transformed his life. Rick was raised by a single mother who left him with his uncles and aunts while she worked. The problem, Rick says, was that "everyone was a dope fiend or a pothead, so eventually I wound up using, myself. I started getting high at the age of eight years old."

He graduated to harder drugs and ended up homeless. "I used to wake up in the streets and eat from garbage cans. I used to ask for quarters, spare change. It was embarrassing. I'd get on the bus and people would look at me in disgust. And I'd want to explain, 'Listen, this isn't me. I'm just going through a phase right now.' But you can't explain something like that." Looking back is not easy. "There have been moments in my life when I wanted to die."

Like Dallas and Devon, Rick's drug habit led to arrest and imprisonment. But the way Rick remembers his time behind bars amazed me. "Prison literally saved me. When I first got arrested and I went away, I felt a sense of relief. 'Thank you. Get me out of this world.' "

In prison, Rick resolved to change his life. He learned to read and write and earned his GED. He saved up the sixteen cents an hour he earned in prison to buy a radio so he could listen to NPR and improve his vocabulary. And he fantasized about what his life would be like if he ever made it out again.

Over time, those fantasies became more concrete. Rick and his best friend, Pete Martinez, wrote letters to fifty different transitional programs. Sixteen wrote them back, offering a bed when the men got out. But the Doe Fund was different. It was the only program that *didn't* promise to give them anything. "They wrote back and said, 'You show up face-to-face, we'll talk, and we'll decide whether or not you're cut out for this program.' "

Impressed, Rick and his friend made a deal. Whoever got out first would go to the Doe Fund and write back each week to update the other. Pete got out first. Sure enough, he gained acceptance into Ready, Willing & Able. He pushed the bucket, built up savings, and earned a pest control license. And Rick used Pete's letters to map out a detailed six-month plan for his life, which he presented to the parole board. They decided to give him a chance.

I first met Rick a week after he arrived at Ready, Willing & Able. It was freezing cold—the dead of winter. He was assigned to his first route pushing the bucket. Later I asked him to look back on that first week. "I was working on the Hudson River, where, when the wind whips, it's twenty degrees below," he says. "I loved it! I was in the world. I was connecting with people. I'd wear the uniform and people would gravitate toward me and ask me questions. I gave directions; I shoveled walkways; I dropped salt. I helped people. I'd done so much damage to the city, terrorizing the people in the city, committing crimes. Now I found myself sweeping and shoveling and helping people. I had people come up to me and say, 'Thank you for what you do.' "

Pushing the bucket is precisely the kind of work progressive society tells us is worse than no work at all. Those people should sit down with Rick Norat.

In a properly functioning free enterprise economy, very few people stay in entry-level positions for long. The same is true at the Doe Fund. Once trainees have pushed the bucket for ninety days, they transfer to one of the organization's revenue-generating businesses. They specialize, receiving particular skills that help them turn jobs into careers. They apprentice in a specific field of their choosing, while also taking classes in financial management, interview skills, and GED preparation if they need it. In the memorable words of one graduate who chose the culinary arts program, "I went from cleaning the gutter to melting the butter."

And nine months after that, the Doe Fund recommends the men for placement with one of their hundreds of employer partners. Today, Doe Fund graduates work as security guards, pastry chefs, auto mechanics, maintenance workers, data entry technicians, home health aides, baristas, butchers, and dozens of other careers. On average, their new jobs pay $10.85 an hour. Many pay much more, some as high as $39 per hour. Rick Norat went into pest control, like his friend Pete.

As we know, the data tell us that money does not buy happiness. So let's forget about the salary and ask what really matters. Are these men happy? Ask Rick Norat that question and he stares back at you for a moment, and repeats the question.

"Am I happy?"

He digs into his pocket and retrieved a brand-new iPhone. I thought he was going to say he was happy because he had an iPhone, and all my theories about attachment would be shot! But no: He opened up his email and pulled up a message from his boss. It was sent that morning, an urgent request for an emergency bedbug job. "They needed someone desperately. Right now. And they called *me*." His speech is slow and deliberate. "I've become a go-to guy for the company. I am *needed*. I have a purpose. Do you understand? These people need me. I've never had that."

This is what the rest of America forgets. This is what people forget when they demean "dead-end jobs." This is what people forget when they buy into the lie that struggling people are just thrilled to rely on government aid instead of their own earnings. And this is what all of us miss who wake up every morning and take "pushing the bucket" for granted.

Work gives people something welfare never can. It's a sense of self-worth and mastery, the feeling that we are in control of our lives. This is a source of abiding joy. There's a reason that Aristotle wrote "happiness belongs to the self-sufficient." The social science bears this out. Studies show that people who receive public support are twice as likely as those not receiving public support to report feeling worthless.[10] "Very happy" people work more hours each week than those who are "pretty happy," who in turn work more hours than those who are "not too happy."[11]

Notice how this is precisely the opposite of what popular culture conveys. We are all supposed to view work as drudgery: Work is a drag. Work is boring. Work is punishment.

Wrong, wrong, and wrong. As we saw earlier, the best data

consistently show that more than eight in ten Americans like or love their jobs. And incredibly, that result holds steady across the income distribution. This notion that "knowledge work" is fulfilling, but everyone who works in a garage or a restaurant loathes his or her life, is an incredible act of condescension masquerading as concern.

The truth is much more egalitarian. Again, economic mobility is crucial, and stagnant wages are a huge problem for American families. But this doesn't change the deep truth that work, not money, is the fundamental source of our dignity. Work is where we build character. Work is where we create value with our lives and lift up our own souls. Work, properly understood, is the sacred practice of offering up our talents for the service of others.

Some don't get this. They see low-wage work as punishment, which is why they oppose work requirements for welfare. And, let's be honest, conservative rhetoric often sounds like we seek to *force* people into the drudgery of work. Both of these approaches are misguided. We don't want to *make* people work. We aim to give every American a shot at the *blessing* of work, to rescue our fellow citizens from the misery of idleness.

Aim at anything less, and we're failing to live up to the example of the Men in Blue.

## LESSON 3. VALUES MATTER MOST IN LIFTING PEOPLE UP.

By sharing the blessing of work, the Doe Fund helps its trainees pull themselves out of material poverty. But it imparts something greater than financial stability. The program helps them learn and live the values that are the sword and shield of a successful life.

In a misguided attempt at compassion, some try to explain away personal failures by making reference to people's brutally tough environments. Who are we to look down at people who make bad decisions, when they are confronting situations far worse than anything we have dealt with?

The call to humility and self-awareness is admirable, as far as it goes. But the underlying presumption here is rotten. At its core, this attitude embodies what Pope Benedict XVI called "the dictatorship of relativism." [12] *Don't judge!* It says that the ethical standards to which we should be held scale up or down according to our salaries. Too often, the message of our bureaucratic society is: If you're poor, you can't be held to the same standards as the well-off. If you slept in Grand Central Terminal, or if your grandmother turned your living room into a crack house, we shouldn't expect you to live an upright life. You don't have to treat people with respect. You don't have to stay sober or provide for your children.

Creating a separate set of moral standards according to socioeconomic status is not an act of mercy. It is a crime against the poor. It is an abdication of our social duty to hold one another accountable. It is shameful that our self-styled elites are so afraid to preach the very secrets to success they so readily practice in their own lives.

Pretend that you were given a choice between leaving your kids a huge trust fund and raising them to have good values. Which would you choose? It's a no-brainer. You'd choose values every time. You know that if your kids have the right values, they don't need the trust fund. They might not get rich, but they are going to earn their own success and be all the happier for it.

When we refuse to hold people to high standards, we aren't taking pity on them. We are robbing them of their opportunity. This is the kind of discrimination that President George W. Bush used to call "the soft bigotry of low expectations." [13] We should find this kind of bigotry intolerable.

The Doe Fund rejects this discrimination. It tells people who can barely keep treading water that they can be held to the same moral standards as anybody else, and they will prosper as a result. The program sets high expectations for every single man who walks through its doors—and challenges them to exceed these standards.

Everyone who chooses to join Ready, Willing & Able is required to sign a contract. The document lays out exactly what is expected of them and what they can expect from the program in return. Each part of the contract reflects core Doe Fund values. The trainees agree to abide by these values. In exchange, the Doe Fund promises to pay, house, and feed them, and to provide work, education, job placement, and graduate services after they depart.

This includes the values of honesty and integrity. Participants must be truthful with others, including staff. There is also the value of orderliness: trainees agree to wear appropriate clothing, maintain personal hygiene, be truthful with staff, and keep their rooms clean.

Recognizing the core value of thrift, the Doe Fund also deducts mandatory savings from their paychecks, which go into a bank account set up for each client. Once they are placed in jobs, they agree to save at least 60 percent of their net earnings. By the time they leave the program after nine to twelve months, these formerly homeless men have a nest egg that they can use to commence their new lives.

Next is the value of personal responsibility. Part of this is agreeing to work every day, and paying a modest rent out of their pay. But this also involves responsibility toward family as well. If they have children, they are required to identify themselves to the city's child support enforcement office. A portion of their checks is then deducted for child support—because living a moral life means providing for your family. "When you leave here," Naz instructs every trainee, "you are going to be the head of a household."

Then there's the value of sobriety. If they want to see those paychecks keep coming, they need to stay clean and sober. No exceptions. Twice a week, the Doe Fund conducts random drug tests. But what happens when someone fails? Is he immediately kicked out of the program?

Worse: The privilege of work is taken away. The man's fellow trainees will start asking, "Hey, why aren't you out there pushing the bucket?" He will have to explain to his friends and colleagues that it's because he started using drugs again. These guys are afraid to lose their income, of course. But more acutely, they don't want to have that conversation. Part of friendships and communities is accountability, a key part of personal responsibility. Just as any of us might select a workout partner whom we don't want to disappoint, positive peer pressure helps lock the Doe Fund trainees into the lifestyles they want to be living.

What is the result of all these values? "They are cognitively being restructured," Naz explains, "whether they realize it or not. Everybody knows that if you do something for thirty days, every day, that's a habit. So we've reversed the addictive process." The Doe Fund gets people hooked on moral values.

When people protest that the Doe Fund expects too much from the homeless, George has a reply at the ready. He testifies that homeless men *want* to be held to high standards. They want to live upright, values-based lives. "Every guy that we get through— every man—what's common is that they want to be fathers to their children. What I hear over and over again is that their father wasn't there for them, and they want to make sure they are there for their son or daughter."

Thanks to the Doe Fund, the Men in Blue can be vectors who pass on good values to their children. As a result, their kids are far less likely to end up on the streets, on drugs, or in jail. In a recent meeting with graduates, George asked, "How many of you when you first came to the Doe Fund considered yourselves role models for the community and your family?" Nobody raised their hand. Then George asked, "How many of you now are role models to your family and community?" And they all raised their hands. That's how they see themselves.

The Doe Fund understands that all the material relief in the world won't build a sustainable life unless it's paired with positive moral values, and the expectation that those values can and must be met, no matter if you are a billionaire or living on the street. That's true nondiscrimination, and the secret to success.

## LESSON 4. HELP IS IMPORTANT, BUT HOPE IS ESSENTIAL.

In the 1960s, a young psychologist named Martin Seligman was conducting experiments on animals when he noticed something curious. The research team he was working on started out by exposing dogs to unpleasant electric shocks that the animals could not escape. Twenty-four hours later, they placed the dogs in a cage where they would again receive shocks—but this time, there was a way out. If the dogs would merely jump over a short barrier into a different section of their cage, the pain would cease. But they could not do it.

In the phrase that Seligman would go on to make famous, the dogs had "learned helplessness." Their futility to stop the first day's shocks had crushed their ingenuity, squelched their spirits, and blinded them to escape routes they would have ordinarily found instantaneously.

The scientists tried removing the barrier so the dogs merely had to step across the cage. But still the dogs refused. They even tried actively guiding the dogs, opening a little window and calling to them—"Here, boy!" But even after all this, half the dogs remained trapped and continued accepting the shocks. It was only when the scientists forcibly led the hapless pooches across the cage that they finally saw the solution.[14]

Human beings can learn helplessness, too, as Seligman found in later experiments.[15] In fact, humans are more vulnerable to learned helplessness, because people are capable of "vicarious learning." They can learn to be helpless by watching other humans encountering uncontrollable events.

George McDonald says that most of the Doe Fund's clients arrive having faced "unimaginable hardships, incredible violence, bleak, soul-crushing circumstances from the time they were just little children." From early ages, they have been conditioned by their own experiences and the hopelessness that surrounds them to believe that they cannot help themselves. That they are destined to lives of poverty and despair. That the "American Dream" is a delusion.

This is why our approach to helping the poor over the past fifty years has been so destructive: It reinforces learned helplessness instead of combating it. Dozens of assistance programs that seem sensible in isolation add up to an overarching message that nobody intended to convey: "You can't do it, so we're going to carry you." That is the last message a person suffering from learned helplessness needs to hear.

The Doe Fund confronts this constantly. Naz asks the men what they really want out of life. "Food stamps?" he asks. "That's all you dream of? That's all you want? You can go wherever you want to go. Are you going to settle?" The Doe Fund teaches the poor not to settle. It helps the homeless help themselves—by replacing learned helplessness with hope.

But what does "hope" mean in this context? Virtually everyone in Washington talks about "hope," but few understand what they're saying. Ordinary Americans know that hope is vitally important, but it can also feel insubstantial and insufficient as a political goal. And when you actually dig into the data, both those instincts prove to be well founded.

After decades of research, psychologists have learned that hope comes in two very different varieties. First, "hope" can be a vague emotional state that is disassociated from practical reality. We *hope* for world peace. We *hope* that the Seahawks make it to the Super Bowl. We *hope* the government will do something nice for us. The problem is, when we talk about "hope" in this way, we're implying that we have no personal say in the matter. We don't "hope" for goals that are actually within our own reach.

This kind of thinking has consequences. If we allow this passiveness into our speech, it creeps deeper into our psyche. Psychologists conduct experiments where they prime people to think about this vague, emotional kind of hope. And afterward, they find, their subjects have reduced feelings of personal control.

The second kind of hope is very different. Call it "practical hope." Instead of a fleeting emotion, psychologists say practical hope is the combination of two mindsets. The first is the belief that a pathway exists between me and my goal—that *it can be done*. The second belief is that I, personally, have the agency to walk down that path—that *I can do it*.

"It can be done" plus "I can do it." This kind of hope affects our thinking, too—but in a much more positive way. Studies demonstrate that practical hope makes happiness and success more likely. Practical hope proves to be an accurate predictor of students' academic performance and of adults' life satisfaction. It even predicts differences in athletic performance that are not explained by the athletes' natural talents.

This research is extremely important for our purposes. When politicians say the government needs to give people "hope," that can mean one of two things—and the two are nearly opposites. On one hand, it can mean removing people's destinies even farther from their own control, persuading them that fixing their lives is somebody else's job. That is the false hope of the last few years—the hope that says, "I sure hope that the government helps me."

But the other kind of hope empowers people. It tells them that a happy life full of meaningful work is within their reach—and that they, personally, can build it. This is the American Dream. This is the restless optimism that built our nation. This is the hope of generations of immigrants who came to America in search of a better life. This is the hope that animates the conservative heart.

The Doe Fund understands this. It infuses the trainees with practical hope. It tells every man that independent living *can be done* and that *he can do it.* That's why, a quarter century after its founding, the Doe Fund has produced 22,000 alumni. That's why it has the reputation that makes it magnetic for so many troubled men. The program replaces learned helplessness with practical hope.

Of course, America's hope shortage is not limited to the homeless. The number of long-term unemployed in America is at record levels today, and dependency on food stamps, Social Security disability insurance, and other government assistance is growing.

America is slipping into the quagmire of learned helplessness. We desperately need a hope agenda for the whole nation. We need to remind every American that *it can be done* and that *they can do it*—and we need to build an economy that lives up to that promise.

## THE AMERICAN DREAM

So there you have it: the formula for the conservative heart, right from the Doe Fund's living laboratory. All we have to do is remember four principles:

1. People are assets, not liabilities.
2. Work is a blessing, not a punishment.

3. Values matter most in lifting people up.

4. Help is important, but hope is essential.

But to put these principles into action, conservatives need to get into the game. We have the secret for lifting people up and helping them lead lives of dignity. Instead of keeping it to ourselves, we need to start sharing that secret with the world. And we can begin by embracing the work of social entrepreneurs like George and Harriet McDonald.

George and Harriet believe these things in their hearts. They don't think the principles that animate the Doe Fund are limited to helping these men; they see them as central to the whole American Dream. "I think we *are* the American Dream," George says. "I put it right on their sleeve. When we designed the uniform, we put a flag on their sleeve. I said I want them to be larger than themselves and part of America."

Richard Norat believes in the American Dream he has learned at the Doe Fund. "My American Dream is to be a part of the society, be a part of the community, to be able to earn a wage, to be able to make money to buy what I want, to live comfortably and not be afraid of someone taking it from me, knowing that I can wake up in the morning and I have a place to go to make my money, to have a job."

America needs to learn from George and Harriet, and the Men in Blue. So does the conservative movement. And you know what? So does the rest of the world. In the next chapter, we will visit a slum in India, a ghost town in Austria, and a few interesting stops in between. In the process, we will see people who inspire and bureaucracy that depresses, and in the process witness a cautionary tale for America that shows just how important it is that the conservative heart prevail.

# Chapter 4

# LESSONS FROM AN INDIAN SLUM AND AN AUSTRIAN GHOST TOWN:

## Inspiration from a Society on the Make and a Cautionary Tale from One That Disappeared

"Ladies and gentlemen, we have encountered a mechanical problem and will be making an emergency landing."

These are never words anyone longs to hear from a pilot. But they were especially unwelcome on the Air India flight I was taking from Colombo, Sri Lanka, to Calcutta, India. I was nineteen years old. A freshly minted college dropout, I was on a concert tour around the world in November 1983 with my brass quintet.

It turned out to be a fairly undramatic landing in the southern Indian city of Chennai. But we were a thousand miles from our desired destination of Calcutta. The phone lines were down countrywide, it was the middle of the night, we knew no one, and we had no place to sleep. After a few hours we lined up a hellhole of a hotel to sleep in and settled in for what was to be two undocumented days next to an Indian slum.

My comrades, older and more sensible than I, had the good sense to stay put in our oven of a hotel. I, on the other hand, set out to explore. What I found shocked me profoundly. I saw poverty I had never encountered before: I saw lepers, malnourished children, and a constant stream of beggars, degraded and desperate.

The whole experience took me back to the *National Geographic* photo of my childhood, and stuck with me for thirty-one years. I'll never forget that specter of human desolation and misery.

Thirty-one years later, I returned to India—this time not as a musician, but as the president of AEI, coming to see what Americans could learn from India's stunning economic transformation. I had seen the data showing life for the very poor in India had improved a lot since I was there in 1983, but I wanted to see with my own eyes. If you study poverty, it is important to meet and speak with actual poor people. That teaches you more than any data point on a spreadsheet.

That is why I had visited the Doe Fund in New York—to meet the Men in Blue and learn how they had overcome homelessness. And that is why I was headed to visit an Indian slum called Dharavi—to meet the people who lived there, to learn how they were lifting themselves up from extreme want, and to witness the true progress brought about by globalization, trade, and entrepreneurship.

## I ❤ DHARAVI

Dharavi is home to more than 700,000 people who live and work in an area about two-thirds the size of Central Park. That yields a density of about 1,300 people per acre.[1] To put that in perspective, the average new single-family home in America is built on a little more than one-third of an acre.[2] So, if you can imagine four hundred people living on your property, you're starting to get the picture.

I have never in my life been in a more crowded place. Every inch of Dharavi is in use. The ramshackle houses are all improvised, one piled on top of the other, built without permission over many years. The buildings are so close together that they block the sun like a rain forest canopy. Even in daytime, the walkways are dark as night. You have to watch your head, but also your feet: There is something undesirable underfoot at all times, from mud to mice to open sewers.

While in Dharavi, I met a family of four who lived in a room the size of my daughter Marina's bedroom. There was no indoor plumbing or furniture—just a single, twelve-square-foot room. By day, the family ate on the floor. At night, they slept on four bedrolls that were stored in the corner. One single electrical outlet was used to power blinking Christmas lights that framed large pictures of Hindu gods and saints. One wall was completely open with a ladder extending down to the street below. This served as their front door.

The children were two and four years old, a boy and a girl. Well-fed and cheerful, they gazed at me with that perplexed, questioning stare I remembered from my own kids when they were little. Who the heck is this weird-looking guy? they were thinking. The parents were in their mid-twenties, having migrated to Dharavi from a rural village in search of work. They were happy to welcome me. Upon leaving, I confessed to my guide that I couldn't imagine a family of four sharing that space. After he finished laughing, he informed me that the last tenants were a group of twelve.

Dharavi is unbelievably hot. Mumbai's famous heat and humidity are only the beginning, supplemented everywhere by open fires. There are fires for cooking, fires for pottery, fires for melting down aluminum and plastic. It feels like everything around you is burning. The morning before, I had looked at the weather forecast and thought I had to be misunderstanding what I saw. It said, literally, to expect "95 degrees and *smoke*." In Dharavi, smoke is a weather forecast.

The heat is only part of the sensory overload. Dharavi is a world of unbelievable smells. It starts with the dense and acrid smoke in the air. Then there are dogs, cats, and goats all around. Roughly 1 percent of Dharavi's residents have their own toilets. The others either use common community toilets, pay toilets (which cost three cents per use), or open-air pits in the slum's outskirts. And the village is loud. Hammering, drilling, grinding, and yelling is the incessant soundtrack.

As anyone who has traveled abroad knows, other societies quickly defy whatever preconceptions we bring along with us. For most Americans, the phrase "inner-city poverty" probably conjures images of degradation, disrepair, and a dearth of industry and work. But I saw none of these things in Dharavi. There is a lot of poverty, to be sure—poverty way beyond anything we are used to in American cities—but little sense of deep deprivation. Everybody is busy. Children are going to school (public school is free; private school is cheap), adults are heading to work, and the whole place is absolutely abuzz.

There is also lots and lots of garbage. This sounds terrible, but it is actually far from the worst possible sign. In the world's most destitute places, there is little garbage. Dharavi is *full* of garbage. Much of its economy is even built on the stuff. Scavengers from Dharavi pore over Mumbai's municipal dumps, gathering plastic, cardboard, glass, wire hangers, cans, car batteries, computer parts—whatever can be found—and bring it all back to the slum to be sorted and recycled. Nothing goes to waste.

I visited a makeshift factory where people were sorting plastic refuse. In one corner, a worker was sorting vast buckets of used toothbrushes. In another, someone was sifting through piles and piles of plastic forks that, they told me, were used on airplanes.

Beside him, someone was sorting plastic milk jugs. The next guy was organizing plastic motor oil containers.

Each type of plastic was separated and sorted. Then, I learned, a machine in the next room grinds the sorted trash into tiny pieces. Teams of workers wash the pieces and dry them in the blazing sun on the roofs of houses. The cleaned pieces are then brought back downstairs, melted in vats, and turned into long strings. Those strings are cut into pellets and sold to make new things out of plastic. I held a handful of these pellets, hot out of the machine.

Recycled plastic from Dharavi is sold across the world. You probably have Dharavi plastic in your home and don't even know it. Perhaps some of the garbage you produce will find its way back there and restart the cycle anew.

That was just one factory. I also visited an aluminum recycler, a pottery factory, and a place where goats are slaughtered and their skins are processed (I know no words capable of describing that particular smell). Dharavi has hundreds of leather manufacturers, plus garment factories, embroidery shops, brass foundries, gold refineries, bakeries (the wares of which I sampled), kite plants, and soap and detergent factories (which recycle discarded used soap from India's luxury hotels). There are at least 15,000 factories here,[3] and 80 percent of Dharavi's residents work inside the slum itself.[4]

Some Westerners might look at Dharavi and feel sorry for all these hopeless people stuck in the drudgery of "dead-end jobs." And of course, we all hope that the residents' lives become easier. Personally, I was expecting to see misery like I encountered thirty-one years before in Chennai.

But I did not. There are still millions of truly poor people in India, but it is simply not the same country as it was in 1983, which was the worst point of its basket-case period. Indira Gandhi's socialism—motivated by a deeply misguided admiration for Soviet communism—was in the process of starving millions. But while I was heading back to college in the 1990s, the winds of change were blowing across the subcontinent. In the past twenty years, poverty in India has been cut by more than half,[5] as free enterprise has pulled some 200 million people out of poverty.[6] Between 1965 and 1975, per capita income in India rose by just 0.3 percent annually. But from 2005 to 2013, that figure more than doubled, from $740 to $1,570.[7] If India continues growing at these rates, it will cease to be a poor country in the next few decades.

As a result, Dharavians are anything but hopeless, and they emphatically do not see their work as fruitless. Despite the over-crowding and terrible sanitation, Dharavi is a magnet commu-nity. Migrants from all over India flee desperately poor villages, pouring into the slum to seize the chance to work. Here they can make money sorting, sewing, or smelting and send much of it back to their families. Everyone I talked to—everyone—told me that Dharavi was on its way up. It is a relentlessly optimistic place.

My guide through Dharavi was a young man named Krishna. He was about thirty years old, with a shaved head—kind of an Indian hipster—and was wearing a T-shirt that said, "I ♥ Dharavi." He meant it. Krishna was born to a poor family in a village outside Bangalore. He came to Dharavi at the age of thirteen to build his own future. He started out serving tea, went to school, and even-tually built a tour business. He now makes about $500 per month. That is big money in Dharavi.[8]

Entrepreneurs like Krishna have built what the *New York Times* calls a "self-created special economic zone for the poor."[9] Dharavi boasts an estimated economic output of between $600 million and $1 billion a year. According to a Harvard Business School study, that makes this unofficial cauldron of entrepreneurship more pro-ductive than many official Special Economic Zones set up by the Indian government.[10]

Make no mistake: Living conditions in Dharavi today are awful by American standards. In even the poorest communities in the

United States, you will find better sanitation and housing than in Dharavi. While there are public and private schools for children, there is also child labor, which no one wants as a long-term solution. Everyone knows the residents deserve better than their current lot.

But Dharavi today, compared to what I saw decades ago, is still nothing less than a miracle. It has gone from a seemingly hopeless place to a vibrant, increasingly prosperous one that is helping to drive a growing country's rapid economic transformation.

Dharavi is on the make. When I left, I had to admit that, well, I ❤ Dharavi, too.

## A VILLAGE THAT IS NO MORE

Unlike Dharavi, I never managed to visit the tiny Austrian village of Marienthal. I have a good excuse, though: Marienthal no longer exists—at least not in the form it once did. And what happened to Marienthal also holds lessons for the future of America if we continue to allow work to disappear and dependence to grow.

In 1929, Marienthal was a thriving factory town twenty miles southeast of Vienna, the nation's capital. It formed in the early nineteenth century around a flax mill, which later grew into a thriving textile factory. By the early twentieth century, the village had 478 families.

The work was hard, but the salaries were ample and community life was rich. Residents socialized with their neighbors, enjoyed the town's manicured parks, and belonged to numerous social clubs. Weekends were dedicated to church, family outings, and evening dances.

But all that changed suddenly in 1932. The town's sole employer went bankrupt. Almost overnight, the factory was shuttered and almost all of Marienthal's families lost their earnings. Two years later, only one in five families in the village still had a member earning income from regular work. The village became a microcosm of idleness and economic depression.

The slow-motion tragedy that unfolded next could easily have been lost to history. Fortunately, a group of young Austrian sociologists were seeking to study how critical levels of unemployment reshaped societies. They knew an ideal case study when they saw it. The researchers descended on Marienthal to watch, listen, and learn from the people who lived there.[11]

So what did they find? First of all, you might imagine that widespread unemployment would lead to extreme financial hardship. It being 1929, you might even expect to see India-like conditions. But that's not what happened. In the years between the world wars, Austria had generous unemployment insurance that covered the better part of a factory worker's wages. But like many social democratic systems of wage replacement, the insurance payments strictly prohibited any work for pay, theoretically to prevent "double-dipping." And it was in the resulting idleness, the researchers found, where the real nightmare started.

First, something strange started happening to the way Marienthal's residents spent their time. With the factory closed but some income still flowing in, people should have had all day to participate in the leisure and social activities they loved. But these activities virtually disappeared. One citizen summed up the paradox: "I used to have less time to myself but do more for myself." Now it was the opposite.

Most of us have heard the old principle that if you want something to get done, you should ask a busy person. Well, when work disappeared, Marienthalers couldn't seem to find the time and energy to do much of anything—even enjoy their new leisure.

"[One] might think that even amid the misery of unemployment, men would still benefit from having unlimited free time," the researchers wrote. "On examination, this leisure proves to be a tragic gift. Cut off from their work," the workers "lost the material and moral incentives to make use of their time." They began to "drift gradually out of an ordered existence into one that is undisciplined and empty. . . . [For] hours on end, the men stand around on the street, alone or in small groups, leaning against the wall of a house or the parapet of a bridge."

"Nothing is urgent anymore," the report observes. "They have forgotten how to hurry."

"It used to be magnificent," one woman told the researchers. "During the summer we used to go for walks, and all those dances! Now I don't feel like going out anymore." Another man summarized, "[T]here was life in Marienthal then. Now the whole place is dead."

Although residents now had unlimited time to read, the town's reading habits collapsed in the two years after the factory shut down. Before, the town library lent an average of 3.23 books to each resident; after, just 1.6. "Since I have been out of work," one man admitted, "I hardly read at all. One doesn't feel like it anymore."

Public spaces began literally falling apart. "Opposite the factory lies a large park," the researchers noted, of which "the people of Marienthal once were very proud." It had boasted beautiful benches and manicured gardens. "Now the park is a wilderness; the paths are overgrown with weeds and the lawns are ruined. Although almost everyone in Marienthal had enough free time, no one looks after the park."

Even Marienthalers' sense of time seemed to warp. Men stopped wearing watches. Wives complained that their husbands were chronically late for meals, even though they were not coming from anyplace in particular. It took people longer and longer just to walk down the street. But interestingly, the researchers found that this phenomenon was different for men and women. The men walked more slowly and stopped more often. The scholars theorized it was because the women were not really unemployed; "they have a household to run which fully occupies their day."

People slept for hours more each night than they ever had. They could not recall how they spent their days, and spent far more time sitting at home or standing around in the street than doing anything else.

Worst of all, the people quickly turned on each other in the face of adversity and idleness. Marienthalers took it upon themselves to enforce the government dictum that nobody could supplement the insurance payments with earned income. One poor soul lost his unemployment benefits after he was turned in to officials by his neighbors for taking a little money while playing his harmonica on the street. Another man lost his benefits after he helped fell trees in return for a share of the firewood. A woman lost her benefits after she delivered milk and was given some for her own children. Any sense of solidarity had been shattered.

Unsurprisingly, for many, family life followed suit. "I often quarrel with my husband," one woman vented, "because he does not care about a thing any longer and is never home." A different husband, describing his wife: "What strangers we are to each other; we are getting visibly harder. Is it my fault that times are bad? Do I have to take all the blame in silence?" Still another woman had even sunk deeper into depression. "I couldn't care less now. If I could hand the children over to the welfare people I would gladly do so."

What decimated life in Marienthal was not the loss of wages. For most, public assistance blunted the financial blow of the layoffs. What destroyed Marienthal was the loss of meaningful work. All the other ills were downstream from this. One man confided in the researchers, "If I could get back to the factory it would be the happiest day of my life. It's not only for the money. Stuck here between one's own four walls, one isn't really alive."

St. Irenaeus once said that "the glory of God is man fully alive." What makes men and women fully alive—what endows them with dignity, happiness, and a sense of self-worth—is work. And the people of Marienthal had lost it.

To be fair, 1929 was a long time ago. Did Europe learn a lesson from this early experience in work-extinguishing policy? Let's move to the present day and see what has happened to modern-day Europe, and the lessons it holds for us here in America.

## LA GENERACIÓN NINI

It is a bit past midnight, but José Luis Flores is not ready for bed just yet. The twenty-three-year-old man living in Cádiz, Spain, simply has too much to do.[12] José begins his evening watching two hours of reality television. When that finishes, he turns to his great passion—video games—which he plays until 4:30 a.m.

How can José live this way at age twenty-three? Won't he be exhausted for work or school in the morning? No and no. He has neither a job nor goes to school. José still lives with his parents.

José is not an anomaly. His case is quite typical and growing more so every day. In Spain, fully one-quarter of people aged 15–29 are neither working nor in school. That's much higher than the average for developed countries.[13] Many young Spaniards between 15 and 29 live with their parents, and few have any plan to move on with their lives. This situation is so common that Spaniards have invented a new nickname. They call this generation *ninis*, short for *la generación nini*: the *nini* generation. That's because they're people who neither work nor study—*ni trabaja, ni estudia*.

*Ninis* are everywhere in Spain. I know several personally. My wife grew up in a working-class neighborhood in Barcelona. *Ninis* are the adult children of her childhood girlfriends, the now-fifty-year-old women who struggle for steady work to support two generations at once. To boot, few of these mothers have ever been married, having come of age in a culture that rejected traditional faith and traditional family life. The fathers of their adult children are nowhere to be found.

But wait: Isn't Spain a happy, traditional, family-oriented Catholic country? It used to be, but church attendance has collapsed by half between 1981 and the present. In 2007, 25 percent of Spanish adults agreed, "Marriage is an outdated institution." [14] According to one survey, nearly 90 percent of Spanish women agree, "It is all right for a couple to live together without intending to get married." [15] Meanwhile, the percentage of Spaniards who feel "very happy" fell by 30 percent between 1981 and 2005.

Meanwhile, the overall unemployment rate for Spanish adults is the highest in Europe—24 percent as of this writing. That catastrophic figure has hardly budged since the trough of the recession in January 2013.[16] And even this top-line figure is dwarfed by the unemployment rate specifically among young adults—it sits at 54 percent. That's a level one would sooner expect from a tinpot dictatorship in total meltdown.

To be sure, regional economic woes play a huge role in all this. But the roots of Spain's malaise reach further down than real estate bubbles and complications with the Eurozone. Recently, the editors of a major Spanish daily newspaper told me that the Spanish embassy in Washington, D.C., had announced what seemed like an exciting new program. The government was offering six hundred paid jobs for young Spaniards to come teach Spanish in America. The initiative seemed like a way to rekindle national pride and create good opportunities for young people who desperately need them. Well, the youth of Spain didn't see it that way. Only three hundred people applied in the entire country.

This is not Marienthal, where economic opportunity was snuffed out and the government stripped your benefits if you were caught working. Here entrepreneurial policymakers actively sought out ambitious young people to fly across the ocean, toward a unique experience and meaningful work as an educator. But something has happened in Spain to make that kind of trip (taxpayer-funded!) seem less attractive than living with mom in Madrid.

And it's not just Spain.

## GRANDMA EUROPE

"I've fallen and I can't get up!"

These words, shouted by an elderly woman, were made famous in a medical alert device ad in the 1990s. In 2015, they are in danger of becoming Europe's catchphrase.

Europe's economic problems are well-known. The recession has come in wave after wave. But if the only issue were macro-economic sclerosis, the problem would be easy to fix. A team of experts could assess the fiscal situation and apply a conventional package of fixes. It might start with monetary and fiscal policy, plus a healthy dose of labor market liberalization. Getting the policy levers and economic incentives right would be sufficient to wrest Europe free from the vortex of decline.

Unfortunately, this is not the answer. As important as sound economic policies are, technocracy will not cure Europe's ailment. This point was articulated beautifully before the European Parliament by none other than Pope Francis. As the Holy Father told his stone-faced audience of European leaders in November 2014, "In many quarters, we encounter a general impression of weariness and aging—of a Europe which is now a 'grandmother,' no longer fertile and vibrant. As a result, the great ideas which once inspired Europe seem to have lost their attraction, only to be replaced by the bureaucratic technicalities of its institutions." [17]

But wait, it gets worse! "Grandma Europe," the pope tells us, is not only tired. She's also going dotty. As Francis sadly explained in an earlier speech to a conference of bishops, she is "weary with disorientation."[18] The continent, in other words, is losing its marbles in addition to its demographic health.

It's important to understand what the Holy Father meant. Pope Francis was hardly going for some kind of cheap shot. He would be the first to remind us that elderly people have great and inherent dignity. Our grandparents grace us with wisdom and experience accumulated over many years of living, thereby enriching the lives of their children and grandchildren.

But this is precisely the sacred duty that "Grandma Europe" has ceased to carry out. Due not to age but to "disorientation," she has lost the ability to recall such honored traditions as faith, family, community, and, especially, work—and thus is unable to share these gifts with new generations. This is the dereliction that led Francis to proclaim that "Europe has discarded its children."

The pope, to be sure, is no demographer. But it is hard to imagine any objective observer objecting to much of his sad appraisal. Take faith, for example. The most diplomatic way to describe the status of religion in Europe is to describe the continent as "post-Christian." Europeans may have some cultural memory of Christianity, but fewer and fewer practice, and many are openly hostile to their religious patrimony.

A 2004 Gallup poll[19] found that just 3 percent of Danes attend church at least once a week. Only 5 percent of Swedes and of Finns do so. Weekly attendance at religious services is below 10 percent in France and Germany, and hovering between 10 and 15 percent in Belgium, the Netherlands, Luxembourg, and the United Kingdom. Spain, an old bastion that many still (inaccurately) view as a cornerstone of European Catholicism, claims weekly church attendance of 21 percent, and much less in major cities like Barcelona. (Some estimates place it under five percent.)

One of the longest holdouts to this secularizing sweep was Roman Catholic Ireland. In 1984, nearly 90 percent of Irish Catholics still made it to Mass every week. But inevitably, Ireland fell as well, and it fell hard. By 2011, that number had plummeted to just 18 percent.[20]

As church attendance has declined, so have birthrates. Europe is indeed becoming barren. The continent's low birthrate has been shrinking its native populations for more than two decades. There are fewer live births in France today than there were under Napoleon. At current birthrate levels, Germany is poised to lose the equivalent of the former East Germany's entire population by 2050, and Spain's population will shrink by one-quarter over the same period.

Imagine a world where most people have no sisters, brothers, cousins, aunts, or uncles. According to Nicholas Eberstadt, a demographer and my colleague at AEI, that's where Europe could head in the coming decades. Birthrates may fall so low that many children's only relatives will be ancestors. Christmas shopping will be more affordable, but that is small consolation for such an unprecedented demographic decline.

There are a few exceptions. France has risen to almost exactly two children per woman in 2012, from 1.95 in 1980.[21] Yet even this exception makes the pope's point: France's increased fertility is widely attributed to a system of government payments to parents,[22] not a change in the culture of family life. Is there anything more dystopian than the notion that population decline can only be slowed when states bribe their citizens to reproduce?

Well, maybe there is. Denmark has taken to airing provocative public service announcements that prod young people to go on holiday and reproduce. The state has been reduced to begging its own citizens to "do it for Denmark!"[23] There is something seriously off about a society where young married couples need their government to encourage them to mate.

If you have spent any time in Europe recently, you know what I mean when I say it feels old. Not the castles, the *people*. According to the U.S. Census Bureau's International Database,[24] a bit more than one in six Western Europeans were sixty-five or older in 2010. This is hard enough to endure, given early retirement ages. But by 2030, this will have risen to more than one in four. That qualifies as science fiction territory for economists.

The effects of current childlessness on the European economy are a disaster in the making. Europe's creaky pension systems operate on "pay-as-you-go" models, meaning that current pensions are paid out of the wages of current workers. That creates quite a problem when your citizens stop replacing themselves. Absent real reform, these systems are vulnerable to insolvency as populations age. There simply will not be enough new workers to pay current retirees' pensions.

And as faith and family have withered in Europe, so has its sense of community. There is so little private charity in Europe that I have a hard time tracking down data. The subject is amply covered in American scholarship, but across the Atlantic, it seems so irrelevant that few researchers bother to investigate it consistently. The best data on private money donations in Europe date from the late 1990s. My adopted country, Spain, has average giving that is less than half that of the United States. Per person, Americans give three and a half times as much as the French, seven times as much as the Germans, and fourteen times as much as the Italians.[25] I would conjecture with confidence that this charity gap has only grown in the intervening years.

What about gifts of time? Data from 1998 compare volunteerism in America and Western Europe. They tell a very similar story. Americans are 15 percentage points more likely to volunteer for religious, political, and charitable purposes than the Dutch, 21 points more likely than the Swiss, and 32 points more likely than the Germans (fewer than one in five of whom volunteer for any causes whatsoever).

Patriotism, another key form of community, is likewise decaying in Europe. Living in Spain, I found it shocking when nobody knew the words to their own national anthem. Nobody stands up when they hear it. The Spanish government had to dig up and begin enforcing a national law requiring public buildings to fly the country's flag. In a small town called Gallifa, officials (Catalan nationalists demanding independence from the Spanish state) complied by putting up a flag "so small it looks like it ought to be attached to a toothpick protruding from a plate of flan." A local leader sarcastically explained himself to journalists: "They are asked for a flag. Well, there it is. I hope they're happy."[26] That would be unimaginable here in the United States—at least for now.

Given all this, you might imagine Spain is an outlier for patriotism in Europe. Indeed it is. But unfortunately, it's an outlier on the *high* end: Spain is actually more patriotic than most of Europe. In 2006, research out of the University of Chicago examined levels of patriotism in 33 countries. According to the *University of Chicago Chronicle*, the study found that "the countries at the bottom of the list are generally established nations in Europe."[27] Nine of the ten least patriotic nations in the world were in Europe: Germany, Latvia, Sweden, Slovakia, Poland, France, Switzerland, and the Czech Republic. Spain came in 17th. Britain trailed at 19th.[28]

## LIVING TO WORK, WORKING TO LIVE

Faith, family, and community are eroding. But the most devastating problem in Europe today—and arguably the root of the others—is the disappearance of work. The percentage of the European population that is in the workforce is withering away.

Again, this is not an isolated problem. In the wake of the recession, work has suffered almost everywhere in the developed world. In the United States, the labor participation rate—the percentage of people who are either working or looking for work—recently reached a thirty-six-year low of just 62.7 percent. Those are disastrous numbers, the worst since the 1970s, and an indictment of our own big government approach.[29]

But as bad as that is, the United States looks swell compared to Europe. The old saying says that Europeans "work to live," while we poor Americans "live to work." That might be compelling if the former group was, you know, actually working. According to the U.S. Bureau of Labor Statistics, in 2012 the labor participation rate in France was 55.9 percent. In Italy it was just 49 percent.[30]

Prolonged unemployment is always a tragedy. It is doubly tragic, though, when it prevents young people from getting a proper start on their adult lives. In America, the unemployment rate for people under 25 is about 12 percent. That's down from an all-time high of 19.6 percent in 2010, but is still much too high.[31] Well, in May 2014, the unemployment rate for those under 25 across Europe was 22.2 percent—almost one in four.[32] In Portugal it was 34.8 percent. In Italy it was 43 percent. And as we already know, in Spain it was 54 percent.

Remember, this is more than a simple shortage of jobs. Macroeconomics are at play, to be sure, but they do not comprise the whole story. As we saw, the Spanish government offered 600 teaching positions and received just 300 applications. It takes a whole worldview to create that level of apathy.

The worldview in question boils down to one word—*retirement*. Getting young Spaniards to take a paid adventure working in a foreign land is like getting your grandmother to do it. She is just too old and too tired to be tempted. In Spain, the whole idea of working hard to reach for new horizons seems to have disappeared. That's a young nation's game. Better, at this late date, to live as comfortably as possible by eating the seed corn—cultural and economic—compiled during previous eras of productivity.

This is why Spain is a nation in decline.

Most readers will have already identified a subject we haven't addressed yet—immigration. Shouldn't the waves of foreigners arriving on Europe's shores buoy our hopes for the continent? In 2012, while the median age of the domestic-born population in the European Union was 41.9, the median age of foreigners living in the EU was 34.7. Presumably, these new arrivals will help stanch the fiscal and demographic bleeding. So, are the Europeans pleased?

Not exactly. Anti-immigrant sentiment is surging across the continent.[33] Nativist movements performed alarmingly well in 2014's European Union elections. By one scholar's count, the number of "far right" anti-immigrant nationalists in the European Parliament has multiplied three and a half times in just five years.[34] One poll found that 69 percent of Italians say immigrants are a burden because they take jobs and social benefits.[35] In Greece it was 70 percent; 52 percent in France; and 46 percent in Spain.

Perhaps "Grandma Europe" is not the best metaphor after all. A tranquil, old grandmother knitting placidly in the window would not be so hostile to newcomers. No, Europe today is more like an angry grandfather, shaking his rake and yelling at outsiders to get off his lawn.

Of course, xenophobia is a terrible outlet for frustration. The problem in Europe is not that the mosques are full on Friday, but that the churches are empty on Sunday. Not that immigrants are having too many children, but that Europeans are barren by choice. Not that foreigners are soaking up all the welfare, but that many Europeans have grown tired of hard work. Not that immigrants are stealing jobs that Europeans are desperate for, but that Europeans themselves have forgotten that work is a blessing.

This European decline has accelerated in recent years, but it had already begun eighty-five years ago in that small Austrian village of Marienthal. Marienthal turned out to be the future of Europe.

And it might be the future of America if we don't change course.

## THREE LESSONS FOR AMERICA

Today, America is somewhere on a continuum between Marienthal and Dharavi—and we are going to have to choose a direction. Some say we should want the castle, not the slum—even if the castle is empty and desolate, while the slum is brimming with work, hope, and opportunity. I understand that. But in focusing on material circumstances, we can make mistakes that risk our future.

The stories of Marienthal and Dharavi—and the data on modern Europe—hold three lessons for us in America.

*Lesson 1. Human dignity is not a function of wealth.*
If you look at Dharavi and see people living in greater degradation and less dignity than someone in Barcelona who has been unemployed for a decade, there is something deeply wrong with your analysis. In a word, it is materialistic. Of course there is breathtaking poverty in an Indian slum. We have a moral duty to relieve it however we can. But in the midst of these people's too-difficult lives, what I saw when I visited Dharavi was *dignity*. What I see when I visit Barcelona is degradation.

This completely breaks the usual materialist frame. Social

democrats in Europe and the United States reduce their vision of dignity to what the lens of economics can capture. In their view, dignity is a quantifiable concept that can be solved by social welfare spending.

Needless to say, I think this cramped thinking gets it exactly backward. Psychologically and philosophically, welfare is no substitute for work. Relieving extreme material want is a necessary step, and we should be thankful our government has the resources to achieve that. But at the same time, a bloated welfare state that nudges middle-class citizens away from the labor force is moving our society away from the dignity of earned success.

## Lesson 2. All honest work is a sanctified pursuit.

Materialism isn't the only reason that someone might view Dharavi as more degraded than Marienthal. Another reason is elitism. Some people simply can't imagine anyone could derive satisfaction from sorting toothbrushes.

We saw this elitist attitude on display when Vice President Joe Biden appeared on *The View* in February 2014 (no, I am not a regular viewer). The vice president took the opportunity to tell women why Obamacare was a blessing: It would give them health care and thus allow them to quit their jobs! "How many of you are single women, with children, in a dead-end job?" Biden asked.[36]

Impressively, this single sentence captures a great deal of what is wrong with elite society. People who have jobs that other elites appreciate look down their noses at people in other positions. They think that anyone whose job doesn't require a lot of higher education isn't really *living* at all—and that government should compensate these poor people so they can quit their undignified toiling.

A few years ago, a *New York Times* reporter interviewed a thirty-nine-year-old Dharavian widow named Sylva Vanita Baskar. She works as a seamstress and earns additional income by renting out her spare room to four laborers. She banks an extra forty dollars a month and lives in the other room with her four children. Through unbelievable thrift, Sylva managed to save several months of her entire salary for a computer to help her kids study. Another several months' salary goes every year to their private school tuition. Her daughter wants to be a flight attendant and see the world. Her son has designs on becoming a mechanical engineer. "The children's lives should be better," Sylva told the reporter with pride. "Whatever hardships we face are fine." [37]

There is incredible dignity in this woman's work. She is building a better life for herself and for her family. She can come home every single day—exhausted, no doubt—and think to herself, *Those children are going to have better lives because of what I do.* She is unlocking new opportunities for them through finances, to be sure. But even more important, she is setting a powerful example. She is modeling values that will enable them to pursue happiness throughout their lives.

Some people just can't see this. They do not see Sylva Vanita Baskar's work as a source of dignity. They see her labor as a punishment. Too many people in positions of power and privilege look down on those who don't make a lot of money, or whose work is deemed boring by the cosmopolitan crowd's standards.

We know better than this. The work of the seamstress in Dharavi is precisely equal in moral standing to the work of a CEO, a think tank president, or the vice president of the United States. A thriving economy creates jobs for all kinds of people at all levels of education and experience. If the ancestors of today's professors had been prohibited from sorting toothbrushes or sewing clothes for the workers' own "benefit," my job would not exist.

Do not misinterpret this. We have a lot more work to do to ensure that the seamstress, the toothbrush sorter, and the McDonald's worker can earn more money for their families. America in 2015 is not a well-oiled machine that churns out real-life Horatio

Alger stories. We must be warriors so that *everyone* can become more prosperous, especially those who need relief the most.

But abundance without the dignity of earned success is a shallow victory, and we must set our sights higher. Pope Francis, noting the youth unemployment rate in Europe, recently asked his fellow European bishops, "What are we doing for the young people? Giving them something to eat? Yes, that's the first thing. But that doesn't give dignity to a young person, to anyone. Dignity comes from work. And there is the danger that the children of Grandma Europe are losing their dignity because they do not have jobs and cannot bring bread home."[38]

The people of Dharavi have that dignity. They are bringing bread home. They are sanctifying their work. If we fail to understand this, we will implement policies that assign insufficient value to jobs for the people who need the blessings of work most of all. We will make America more like Marienthal.

## Lesson 3. It's not where you start out that defines you. It's where you are going.

A dynamic society defines itself by where it is going and what it is doing. A static society defines itself by where it is now. In the last chapter, we saw that Dharavi is a dynamic society. The Europe that spawned Marienthal and modern-day Spain is increasingly static.

Even poor Europeans live in nicer homes than people in Dharavi. But the people of Dharavi don't define themselves by the walls around them. They define themselves by the future they are building for themselves and their children; by the values they are passing on to their children; by the strong bonds of faith, family, and community that they work to strengthen every day.

Dharavi itself is, literally, a place for people who go places. Most of the residents have moved from poor villages all over rural India. They willingly migrate to live in a crowded and sometimes dizzying slum. Imagine the courage this requires—and the determination to be defined not by where you are, but by where you are going. That's the mantra of the migrant. That has historically been the mantra of America.

Throughout our history, America has been a bright beacon for such stories. Our moral example and the economic system we propagate have played an enormous role in building present-day Dharavi. But if we borrow Grandma Europe's amnesia and forget our own lessons, Marienthal will be our future.

So where are we? Whether we visit a homeless shelter in New York, a ghetto in Washington, D.C., a slum in India, or an unemployed village in Austria, the lessons for the conservative heart remain the same. We have a duty and privilege to help those with less power than we have. And *we* need *them* to remind us of the dignity of all work, and the importance of progress.

The agenda for accomplishing this involves a culture of faith, family, community, and work. It requires a little bit of help from all of us. And it requires a nation built on real hope.

This agenda has a name. It is called social justice.

# Chapter 5

# A CONSERVATIVE SOCIAL JUSTICE AGENDA:

## A Better Way to Fight Poverty

Jestina Clayton came to America in 2000 as a refugee escaping Sierra Leone's brutal civil war. Her name, "Jestina," means "justice" in her home country.[1] But what Jestina found when she tried to start a business in America was anything but justice.

Jestina moved to Utah in search of a better life. Looking for a way to help support her growing family while her husband went to school, she saw an opportunity: There were a number of parents in Utah who had adopted African children, but did not know how to braid their hair. Growing up in Sierra Leone, Jestina had learned the art of traditional African hair braiding. She had been braiding hair since she was five years old. And so, like countless American entrepreneurs before her, Jestina came up with an idea to tap into this unserved market: She would start an African hair-braiding business for these adopted children.

It was not long before word spread among parents, and her

business took off. "It's not like it was bringing me millions," she told National Public Radio, "but it was covering groceries."[2]

Jestina Clayton was an American success story. She had escaped a terrible situation, come to the land of freedom and opportunity, and founded a little business that, while not making her rich, was allowing her to help take care of her family. She was building her life. That is the American Dream, right?

Not surprisingly, Jestina was shocked when she received an email from a stranger who warned her, "It is illegal in the state of Utah to do any form of extensions without a valid cosmetology license." The sender threatened to report her to the authorities if she did not stop braiding hair.

Jestina had thought that in America, all you needed to start a business was a good idea and the willingness to work hard to earn your success. So she was stunned to discover that she needed a cosmetology license from the government requiring 2,000 hours of classes costing $16,000. She would have to study 40 hours a week for 50 weeks to do something she already knew how to do. Worst of all, not one single hour of the required training was in African hair braiding. The license had nothing to do with her business.

Jestina was sure that if she explained her unique business to the state cosmetology board, they would see the absurdity of the situation. She was not using any chemicals or equipment that required training. She was just braiding hair. She came to the board with a PowerPoint presentation, explained her business, and asked for an exemption. They turned her down, and told her that she had two choices—get the required training or get the state legislature to change the law. Their solution was to ask a war refugee, new to our country and trying to start a new business, to lobby the state legislature.

Jestina had hit a dead end. She was forced to close down her business—eliminating the source of income she had built for her family, as well as a useful service needed by these adoptive families.[3]

That might have been the sad end of the story, had it not been for the Institute for Justice, a nonprofit public interest law firm devoted to individual rights and economic liberty. The institute heard about Jestina's plight and stepped in to help her. Together, they sued the state of Utah. They argued that the required 2,000 hours of training was more than is required to become an armed security guard (36 hours), a mortgage loan originator (60 hours), or an emergency medical technician (130 hours) *combined*. And in 2012, a federal judge ruled in Jestina's favor. The court declared that "to premise Jestina's right to earn a living by braiding hair on [Utah's licensing] scheme is wholly irrational and a violation of her constitutionally protected rights."

"The system works," Jestina declared after the ruling.[4]

Well, sometimes. Jestina was lucky that a powerful public interest law firm took up her cause, but not everyone who faces the brick wall of government regulation has those kinds of resources at their disposal—especially not the poor. Most people in Jestina's situation just give up.

And Jestina's situation is not unique. Consider: If you want to start a licensed real estate business in Washington, D.C.—a typical second career for upper-income families—you need 135 hours of training.[5] A well-to-do mom can afford a babysitter to take care of the kids while she puts in those reasonable hours. But if you want to start a business painting nails or braiding hair in our nation's capital—a typical first income for poor, single mothers without an education—you need 1,500 hours of training to receive your license.[6] When it is harder to become a hair braider than a real estate agent in America's capital city, the system is officially rigged against people at the bottom.

Jestina was one of the lucky ones. Millions of Americans without her drive, grit—and the help of a law firm—have little hope to rise in America. Currently, all they are offered are promises that the government will stick it more to the rich through higher taxes and greater redistribution. But this will never help a poor American climb out of poverty, find a better job, and get a good education—let alone start a business.

We need real solutions to give those in need the social justice they deserve.

## WHAT IS "SOCIAL JUSTICE"?

Many conservatives recoil at the mere mention of "social justice." They see the term as the exclusive language of the left. But this is a mistake. "Social justice" simply means working for a society that lives up to our American standards of fairness. And conservatives believe in fairness just as much as liberals do. We just define it differently.

The left generally espouses the idea of "redistributive fairness." Liberals argue that beyond some unspecified limit, an uneven distribution of income is unfair on its face, and so promoting social justice means using government to promote greater financial equality for its own sake.

Conservatives, on the other hand, champion "meritocratic fairness." We believe that real fairness means that everyone should have abundant opportunity to pursue their happiness, and that—above a reasonable safety net for the truly indigent—rewards should follow hard work and merit.

Put another way, the left advocates greater equality at the finish line. Liberal efforts to attain social justice, then, usually attempt to equalize outcomes through redistributive taxation and social welfare spending that extends far above the poverty level.

To conservatives, a social justice agenda means making the starting line more equal for the vulnerable by improving education, expanding the opportunity to work, and increasing access to entrepreneurship. Then it must ensure that rewards reflect effort, merit, and virtue. Further, true conservative social justice must also fight cronyism that favors powerful interests and keeps the little guy down.

And what are the policy specifics of conservative social justice? These come from listening to the people who need our help. That's what I was doing in Dharavi and at the Doe Fund.

Strangely, this approach seems to be a rare one. Most research on poverty is performed with actual people nowhere in sight. One of my colleagues tells an instructive story. One afternoon, as he toiled at his PhD dissertation in a top university's poverty research center, an actual poor person walked in. He had seen the signs on the building and thought they could do something to help him. The expert researchers had no idea what to do. Their instinct was to call security.

There is no substitute for hearing what people who have actually lived through tough times have to say—people like Nazerine Griffin, Devon Greene, and Richard Norat, people who once slept on the streets and are now working and earning their own success. They told me precisely what people who are struggling need to build prosperous and satisfying lives. They'll tell you that it was three things that helped them rebuild their lives: good values, a little bit of help, and a whole lot of hope.

It is on these three pillars—values, help, and hope—that conservatives can build the specifics of the social justice agenda that America deserves.

## VALUES

The problem with conventional government approaches to poverty is that many of them unwittingly give up on people. As we learned from the example of the Doe Fund, this flows from a lack of belief in the poor. As individuals and as a society, we often treat poor people as less capable than others of leading productive lives.

By now, everyone acknowledges that poverty in America is often intertwined with social pathologies, such as substance abuse, criminality, domestic violence, and other problems. Values thus play a pivotal role in determining whether people live in prosperity or poverty. According to an analysis by scholars at the Brookings Institution, adults who finished high school, gained employment, and waited until they were at least twenty-one and married before having children had just a 2 percent chance of living in poverty. Their odds of moving into the middle class were better than 70 percent. Those who did not follow that sequence had a 77 percent chance of living in poverty and just a 4 percent chance of reaching the middle class.[7]

Moreover, the Brookings research shows that the decline of marriage and the growth in out-of-wedlock births dramatically increases people's chances of living in poverty. Today, 40 percent of babies born to young women who have a high school degree or less education are born outside of a marriage, making it four times likelier those children will live in poverty. By contrast, if the same share of adults were married today as in 1970, that fact alone would reduce poverty in America by more than a quarter.

Are these problems a cause or a consequence of poverty? Some on the left insist they are symptomatic, and that ramping up income redistribution and government spending programs would help clear these issues away. A few on the right declare that these moral issues are the only ones that matter, and material poverty would vanish if individuals would simply reform their ways.

The truth is more complicated: Values and economics are intertwined. Both common sense and the testimony of the poor themselves tell us values always matter, and that moral intervention must accompany economic intervention for the latter to be truly effective.

This is, as we've learned, why the Doe Fund has been so successful in transforming the lives of homeless men in New York City. Paying child support is a must. Start using drugs again and work is taken away until you get clean. These ethical standards are nonnegotiable. The Doe Fund is strict, but it is precisely through that rigor that it never gives up on people. If they slip up, it helps them back up. But it never stops holding everyone to the same high moral standards.

The key lessons are no different from the lessons that good parents teach their children. Don't use drugs, stay in school, work hard, save your money, be responsible, don't have kids until you graduate and get married, and live an upstanding life—or else the odds will be stacked against you. I've never met a parent who believes that their kids have to receive their allowance before it is fair to ask them to behave decently. It's the other way around!

So why are these values good enough for our children, but not good enough for our brothers and sisters in need? When we fail to share our values with the poor, we effectively discriminate against them. And that hidden bigotry robs them of the tools they need to live lives of dignity and self-reliance.

By the way, this is emphatically not a question that is limited to particular racial or ethnic groups. As my AEI colleague Charles Murray shows in his research, the same problems and pathologies afflict poor white people as other impoverished communities. All of the best research on the topic shows that this is a question of economic marginalization and the associated deleterious social effects.

Many elites today presume that low-income Americans are somehow unworthy of the same cultural principles to which we hold ourselves and our own families. We are told that it is unfeeling and unkind to hold everyone to the same standards, regardless of how much money they make. But in fact, it is condescending relativism that is unfeeling and unkind. Conservatives must promote and defend the time-tested stores of personal and social meaning—faith, family, community, and earned success through work—for everyone.

## A LITTLE BIT OF HELP

The number of Americans who are genuinely needy is growing. A 2010 analysis from the National Center on Family Homelessness found that child homelessness spiked by a staggering 38 percent during the Great Recession years.[8] And a team of public health researchers stunned readers of the journal *Health Affairs* in 2012 when they released new life expectancy findings. Even as medical advances have increased the average national life span, the scholars found that low-income white females with fewer than twelve years of education have actually seen their life expectancy drop—and sharply—since 1990.[9]

In addition to cutting short life expectancy, poverty also inhibits brain function. In 2013, the *Washington Post* described the results of a study published in the journal *Science*[10]: "[p]overty consumes so much mental energy that people struggling to make ends meet often have little brainpower left for anything else, leaving them more susceptible to bad decisions that can perpetuate their situation. Poverty is the equivalent of pulling an all-nighter," one of the researchers explained. "Picture yourself after an all-nighter. Being poor is like that every day."[11]

Another equally troubling study found that being raised in poverty actually measurably diminishes brain activity in children, starting at a very young age. As soon as early infancy—

well before, I would note, oft-discussed solutions like free pre-K or Head Start would kick in—a lack of opportunity and earned success in a baby's family diminishes how well their brains can work.[12]

Conservatives who are moved by these facts naturally reach for their checkbooks—and deliver in a big way. Here are a few facts about charitable giving I found while researching my 2006 book, *Who Really Cares*:

- Households headed by a "conservative" give, on average, 30 percent more dollars to charity than households headed by a "liberal."[13]
- This discrepancy is not an artifact of income differences. On the contrary, the average liberal family earns an average of 6 percent *more* per year than the average conservative family, yet still gives less away. Conservative families gave more than liberal families within every income class, from poor to middle class to rich.
- These differences go beyond money. Data from 2002 suggest that people who identified as "conservative" or "extremely conservative" made up less than one-fifth of the population but provided more than a quarter of all blood donations. If liberals and moderates gave blood like conservatives do, the blood supply in the U.S. would instantly jump by about 45 percent.[14]

Clearly, conservatives are generous with their own money. But we also know that we cannot solve all problems of poverty and need through private charity. We can and should give even more, and must continue to lead by example. But even in this remarkably charitable country—where voluntary giving alone exceeds the total gross domestic product of nations such as Israel and Chile—

private donations cannot guarantee anywhere near the level of assistance that vast majorities of Americans across the political spectrum believe is our moral duty.

Consider that the total that Americans give annually to human service organizations to assist the vulnerable comes to about $40 billion.[15] Now suppose that we could spread that sum across the 46.5 million Americans receiving food assistance, with zero overhead and complete effectiveness. It would come to just $860 per person per year.

Or take the incredible donation levels that followed Hurricane Katrina in 2011. The outpouring of contributions exceeded $3 billion, a record-setting figure that topped even the response to the attacks of September 11, 2001.[16] But even this historic episode raised enough to offset only 3 percent of the costs the storm imposed on the devastated areas of Louisiana and Mississippi.[17]

Voluntary charity simply cannot get the job done all on its own. That is why we need a government safety net—and why most conservative leaders and thinkers have defended the safety net for the indigent.

Not so sure of that last claim? Here is a pop quiz: Who wrote the following words?

*There is no reason why in a society which has reached the general level of wealth ours has attained [some] security should not be guaranteed to all without endangering general freedom . . . some minimum of food, shelter, and clothing, sufficient to preserve health and the capacity to work, can be assured to everybody. Nor is there any reason why the state should not assist the individuals in providing for those common hazards of life against which [few] can make adequate provision.*[18]

Was it Franklin Roosevelt? Ralph Nader? Senator Elizabeth Warren? Not by a long shot. It was the iconic conservative libertarian economist Friedrich Hayek. That passage is featured in his seminal free market text, *The Road to Serfdom*. And Hayek is not alone in his support for the social safety net for the truly poor and needy. Here's another:

*We're a humane and a generous people and we accept without reservation our obligation to help the disabled, the aged, those unfortunates who, through no fault of their own, must depend on their fellow man.*[19]

That's Ronald Reagan, talking about the safety net in his inaugural address as governor of California.

Hayek and Reagan recognized the moral truth that a real social safety net is one of the great achievements of our free market system. Free enterprise has made America so prosperous that, as a society, we can afford to take care of our brothers and sisters who simply cannot take care of themselves—and to provide temporary help to those who are down on their luck and need a hand up.

Hayek and Reagan also easily distinguished between "some minimum of food, shelter, and clothing"—a core safety net for the truly indigent—and the sprawling, rent-seeking tangle that is today's welfare state. This is why the right must champion a true, sustainable safety net while condemning an ever-expanding system for redistributing income more broadly and establishing greater state control over the economy.

That is precisely what Reagan went on to say in his inaugural address. "We seek reforms," he explained, "that will, wherever possible, change relief check to paycheck. . . . This is not being done in any punitive sense, but as a beginning step in rehabilitation to give the individual the self-respect that goes with performing a useful service." This was essential, Reagan said, because "[t]here is no humanity or charity in destroying self-reliance, dignity, and self-respect . . . the very substance of moral fiber."

Pope Francis made the same point recently about the importance of work to human dignity: "There is no worse material poverty, I would emphasize, than that which makes it impossible to earn a living and deprives someone of the dignity of work." [20]

The pope knows and the future president Reagan knew that a welfare check cannot replace a paycheck. This is why, even as we support a strong social safety net, we must help as many as possible escape it. Conservatives must stand proud as the only force in American politics that simultaneously defends a sustainable safety net for people in genuine need and works hard to make it unnecessary.

Unfortunately, America is headed in just the opposite direction today. Our entitlement programs are becoming more and more central to people's lives, and less and less financially sustainable. Since January 2009, the number of Americans receiving food stamps has increased by 45 percent. And millions more are on the edge of the precipice. Between 2009 and 2011, nearly one in three Americans slipped below the poverty line for at least two months.[21] At this moment, nearly half the country is living paycheck to paycheck, without enough savings to get by if they lose their jobs.[22]

The reason for this is not some novel desire for dependency. Americans did not abruptly start raising their children to hope that one day, when they grew up, they could depend on government to eke out a subsistence-level income. As we have seen, the reason for growing dependency in America is the lack of opportunity for those at the bottom.

So what is the proper conservative response to this growing problem of dependency? Here is the wrong answer, and one that some conservative leaders advocate: Cut food stamps!

Trying to reduce dependency by taking aim at relatively uncontroversial pieces of the core safety net is both a moral and political mistake. Most poor Americans don't want to be on food stamps.

They want to work. They simply can't find jobs in an environment when unemployment levels among poorly educated, low-skilled workers rival the worst of the Great Depression. And millions more are walking an economic tightrope, not currently poor but constantly worried that they might slip and fall. When some conservative politicians vote to cut food stamps—which are not a significant long-term deficit driver by any means—these Americans see conservatives snipping away at the safety net below them.

Instead of cutting the safety net, conservatives should be the guardians who protect it, limit it to the truly indigent, and infuse it with work. This entails fiscally conservative policies designed to prevent insolvency and austerity. The largest long-term threat to the core safety net is not wild-eyed conservative budget-cutting, but rather out-of-control entitlement spending on programs for people who aren't really poor. The unchecked fiscal profligacy that some on the left cheerlead may leave us unable to fund even the most fundamental parts of the safety net for those who truly need it.

Doubt it? Look at Europe's suffering periphery. When an economic meltdown left Greece no choice but to cut spending dramatically, the subsequent austerity hit the poor hardest. In 2012, the world was shocked when a seventy-seven-year-old retired pharmacist shot himself in the head in the central square of Athens, leaving a note saying that he could not bear the idea of "scavenging in dustbins for food and becoming a burden to my child." His note blamed austerity measures that shrank the social safety net.[23]

This tragedy was not an isolated incident. The *New York Times* reported in 2012 that "the number of suicides reported in Greece over the past three years has risen sharply, a trend experts attribute to repercussions of the debt crisis, including rising unemployment, now at 21 percent, and deepening poverty."[24] Other reports found similarly alarming trends in homelessness and food insecurity across the Eurozone, as the most vulnerable people suffered the most in the wake of austerity. The lesson is clear: Fiscal profligacy risks insolvency, which results in austerity, which in turn leads to the shredding of the social safety net for those who actually need it.

We cannot put poor people at such risk. Wasting money on foolish domestic boondoggles, on special subsidies to corporations with special access, and on entitlements for people who don't actually need them is no longer a viable option. It's easy to promise a safety net. But committing to one and then actually seeing it through? That takes fiscal discipline, here and now.

That's real compassion—and real conservatism.

To summarize, the conservative orientation toward the safety net should have three key parts. First, as we all know, there is nothing wrong in concept with true safety net programs targeted at genuinely needy people. The implementation of SNAP, housing supports, and Medicaid are certainly imperfect, but their existence is nothing to regret. Americans should take pride in a limited, sustainable net that helps our most vulnerable neighbors. Second, however, these policies absolutely must be designed, administered, and adjusted to help those truly in need, not the rest of us. Third, the safety net's ultimate purpose cannot be to make some Americans' perpetual subsistence in poverty a slightly less miserable experience. Our goal must be to help the poor lead lives of dignity, independence, self-reliance, and above all, work.

## A WHOLE LOT OF HOPE

There are two very different kinds of help. There is help that destroys hope and help that engenders it. Many government initiatives accidentally promote the wrong kind. Too often, the material relief supplied by government implicitly tells its recipients, "You can't do it, so we are going to carry you."

Our message to the poor must be precisely the opposite. We need to convey the constructive, practical kind of hope that we learned about in the last chapter: "It can be done—and *you* can do it." And delivering this message in earnest requires the third plank in the new right's social justice agenda: opportunity.

Conservatives already think of opportunity as the sine qua non of our cause. Nothing inspires us more than a Horatio Alger story, a tale of someone who started with nothing and climbed to the top. Therefore, I submit, nothing should trouble the political right more than the fact that the ladder of socioeconomic opportunity seems to be losing its lowest rungs.

How can a conservative social justice agenda reverse these trends and expand hope and opportunity for all? An opportunity society has two basic building blocks. First is an education system that creates a base of human capital. Second comes an economic system that rewards hard work, merit, innovation, and personal responsibility. So conservatives must passionately advance education reform and relentlessly work for a free enterprise that is accessible to every American.

Meaningful progress toward social justice cannot be made in sclerotic education systems that put adults' job security before children's civil rights. The centuries-old model that governs American schools too easily resists the innovations that upgrade the rest of the economy.

Per-pupil federal education spending has skyrocketed to nearly three times its 1970 level, according to data compiled by Andrew Coulson of the Cato Institute.[25] What has this massive inflow of new resources bought us? A sizable increase in our school systems' employment rolls—but no detectable increase in our children's test scores in reading, science, or math.

And this fecklessness is not evenly spread across America. Our broken bureaucracies systematically ship the very worst product to our most vulnerable kids. Washington, D.C., consistently ranks near the top in per-pupil education spending, yet only half of the city's public school students are proficient readers.[26]

Similar stories characterize cities all around the country with poor populations. And anyone who believes that a barely literate high school dropout is running a fair race in America is deluding himself. If you don't start out with a decent education—if you were never taught adequately to read and write or add and subtract—you are starting the race of life hundreds of yards behind and are very unlikely to be able to get ahead. Equally delusional is many politicians' blind faith that funneling more dollars into the existing statist apparatus is not just heaving more money down the well.

It's not as if we have no idea how to improve this situation. Decades of research and experimentation have shown how charter schooling, vouchers, and other innovations can benefit needy children. In one rigorous study, scholars from Harvard and the Brookings Institution found that school vouchers in New York City significantly increased the proportion of African American students who went on to attend college.[27] Research from Stanford shows that access to charter schools reduced New York City's black-white achievement gap by 66 percent in reading and a stunning 86 percent in math.[28] A Harvard economist has found that Boston's charters produce similarly massive improvements.[29]

My AEI colleague Frederick Hess has spent decades reviewing these results, and his conclusion is unambiguous: "For poor parents trapped in dangerous and underperforming urban school systems . . . school choice works."[30]

Similarly, we have a wealth of information on the best ways to teach disadvantaged children and recruit, retain, and reward the best teachers. In one recent study, prominent economists from Harvard, the University of Chicago, and the University of California, San Diego found that creative ways of linking teacher pay to student performance can push up test scores among working-class students.[31]

Why do these and countless other lessons go unheeded on a national scale? If we know that school choice and pay-for-performance work, why aren't we implementing these solutions everywhere? Simple: They upset the status quo. In California, more than 295,000 teachers and nearly 25,000 administrators work in a K–12 education sector that consumes more than 40 percent of the state's entire general fund.[32] Fundamental, disruptive innovation might mean a significant inconvenience for a huge number of well-organized grown-ups. And by definition, the families and communities who would stand to benefit the most have little time and money to spare on costly political battles.

This is a classic public-choice problem. Only a crusade for social justice will stand a chance at winning this fight. The public schools in this country are failing millions of kids. Are we going to be the generation that tolerates this? Are we going to continue to tolerate school systems that put the interests of adults ahead of children?

Next, there's higher education. America's stiff, one-size-fits-all college system stands in the way of success for too many young Americans.

Between 2006 and 2011, the median inflation-adjusted household income fell by 7 percent. The average real tuition at public four-year colleges increased by more than 18 percent during that period.[33] The average tuition for just one year at a private university in 2011 was almost $33,000.[34] While America has been fix-ated on the costs of health care, college costs have been increasing about twice as fast.[35]

Ballooning student loan debt, an impending college bubble, and a return on the bachelor's degree that is flat or falling: All these things scream out for entrepreneurial solutions. One idea gaining currency is the $10,000 college degree—the so-called 10K-BA—which apparently originated with a challenge to educa-tors from Bill Gates, and which governors in Texas, Florida, and Wisconsin have begun trying to make a reality.[36]

Most 10K-BA proposals rethink the costliest part of higher education—the traditional classroom teaching. Predictably, this means a reliance on online and distance learning alternatives. And just as predictably, this has stimulated antibodies to uncon-ventional modes of learning. Critics dismiss it as an invitation to charlatans and diploma mills.

As an editorialist in the *Chronicle of Higher Education* put it, "No PowerPoint presentation or elegant online lecture can make up for the surprise, the frisson, the spontaneous give-and-take of a spirited, open-ended dialogue with another person."[37] And what happens when you excise those frissons? In the words of the president of one university faculty association, "You're going to be awarding degrees that are worthless to people."[38]

I understand the concerns, but I disagree. You see, I happen to possess a 10K-BA of my own. I got it way back in 1994. And getting that unconventional degree was the most important pro-fessional move I ever made.

In earlier chapters I recounted how I bailed out of college to play music, and then parachuted back in during my late twen-ties, studying by correspondence. At the time, Ester and I had a thin-to-nonexistent bank account and no desire to start our family with a mountain of student loans. Thanks to a virtual education at Thomas Edison State College, I got my whole degree, including the thirdhand books and a sticker for the car, for about $10,000 in today's dollars. I took the same exams as in-person students, but they were proctored at local libraries. I never met a teacher or sat in a single class.

Did I earn a "worthless degree"? Hardly. My undergraduate years may have been bereft of "frissons," but I wound up with a great career. I followed up my 10K-BA with a 5K-MA at a second-tier public university while continuing to work full-time. Finally, it was time to go mainstream, and I earned a standard PhD while working part-time. The final tally for a guy in his thirties helping to support his family: one bachelor's, one master's, one PhD, and exactly zero debt.

My zigzag path cut a few corners, of course. There are plenty of things I missed that I could have gotten at Harvard or Princeton. But if the only option on the table had been traditional universities, I would have had absolutely no shot at higher education. My life would have turned out completely differently.

Years after finally earning that degree, I wrote about my unconventional educational journey in the New York Times. The president of Edison read the story and called me up, offered me an honorary doctorate, and asked me to speak at the school's commencement ceremonies in New Jersey. I jumped at the chance. It would be my first physical visit ever to my alma mater.

I took my middle son, Carlos, along for the trip. He was thirteen at the time. To show their hospitality, the college put me up in Princeton instead of Trenton. Princeton is a wealthier, more picturesque town containing arguably the nation's finest university.

The next morning's commencement ceremony in the Trenton ice hockey arena painted the starkest possible contrast to the night before. The night before, we'd seen elite America; today, hundreds of working-class adults who had worked their tails off to graduate crossed that stage. Half were minorities. Many were active military. A majority were over thirty years old.

The mood was jubilant. One woman captured it perfectly when she stated her name and exclaimed, "I am so grateful for this day, and I want to thank my five children and the Son of the Living God!"

These people—my fellow Edison graduates—taught Carlos a more succinct lesson than I could ever hope to. These people, whom I had never met, were the embodiment of the values my wife, Ester, and I have tried to impart. They refused to take their environment as a given. There was no privilege or elitism. There was just hope, hard work, earned success—and fierce dedication to building their own lives in their own way.

We need to empower many more to share in that success. We need to help more Americans find affordable and meaningful ways to sharpen their talents and build better lives.


Education reform is just the first battlefield. Once equipped with an education that gives them adequate human capital to earn their success, Americans then deserve a hopeful economic system that makes that earned success possible on the widest imaginable scale.

Only the free enterprise system fits the bill. Conservatives can and must champion this truth without apology or compromise. For the sake of all people, our end goal must be to make free enterprise as universally accepted and nonpartisan as civil rights are today.

We have already discussed the hope-crushing barriers to entrepreneurship for those at the bottom of America's economy. The data for overall entrepreneurship are equally bleak: According to Gallup, in 2008, for the first time in thirty-five years, the death rate for American business was larger than the rate of new business births.[39] Until then, new business start-ups had outpaced business failures by about 100,000 per year. For the past seven years, business failures have outpaced new start-ups by about 70,000 a year.

And it's not as if ordinary employees are making out all right and it's only entrepreneurs who are hurting. Working-class people are still in recession, years after its technical end. The bottom 20 percent of U.S. households saw their incomes decline 7 percent, on average, from 2009 to 2013.[40]

This helps explain a particularly unsettling trend. As recently as 2007, fully 70 percent of Americans were satisfied with their opportunities to get ahead by working hard; only 29 percent were dissatisfied. Today, that gap has shrunk to 54 percent satisfied and 45 percent dissatisfied.[41] In just a few years, we have gone from seeing our economy as a real meritocracy to viewing it as something closer to a coin flip.

Faced with all these terrible statistics, some politicians shove aside free enterprise solutions and reach instead for an old favorite to increase incomes—raising the minimum wage. California, New Jersey, and eleven other states recently raised their state minimum wages. The Council of the District of Columbia recently approved a massive increase from $8.25 to $11.50 that will be phased in by 2016. And in 2014, President Obama signed an executive order to raise the minimum wage to $10.10 for the individuals working on new federal service contracts, and called on Congress to raise the national minimum wage from $7.25 to $10.10 an hour. As the president put it in his 2014 State of the Union address, it's time to "give America a raise."

Obviously the president's intent is not to kill half a million jobs, but that is what the Congressional Budget Office says the proposed minimum wage hike would do. And the jobs killed would be precisely those held by the poorest and most marginalized workers with the most tenuous grip on their employment.

Researchers at the University of California, San Diego,[42] studied the effects of a series of recent hikes in the federal minimum wage that raised it from $5.15 in July 2007 to $7.25 in July 2009. Here is what they found:

> *[M]inimum wage increases reduced the employment, aver-age income, and income growth of low-skilled workers over short and medium-run time horizons . . . [and] significantly reduced the likelihood that low-skilled workers rose to what we characterize as lower middle class earnings. . . . The re-duction was particularly large for low-skilled workers with relatively little education. . . . This period's minimum wage increases may thus have made the first rung on the earnings ladder more difficult for low-skilled workers to reach.*

The simple fact is that, like most policies, minimum wage in-creases create winners and losers. The winners tend to be those who don't need the help, including many second earners in middle- and upper-income households. Think of a minimum wage hike as a raise for my teenage kids. Only about 11 percent of the workers who would gain from a minimum wage hike live in poor households. More than 40 percent live in households with incomes at least three times the poverty threshold.[43]

Meanwhile, the losers are those who have the hardest time finding and keeping jobs: the very poor, the disabled, those who are inexperienced, and those with little education. One poignant story from Bloomberg News profiled disabled adults who loved their jobs with nonprofit contractors who perform services for the federal government.[44] President Obama's decision to raise the minimum wage for federal workers is forcing some of these marginalized men and women out of the work they treasured. For them and for untold others, minimum wage increases make the already slippery bottom rung of the labor market ladder even harder to grasp.

As I write this, the African American teenage unemployment rate is about 33.2 percent. One in three of the black teenagers ages 16–19 who are trying to find jobs cannot find them.[45] Now, imag-ine that someone put forward a public policy proposal that would reduce opportunity among urban minority youth even further, in order to provide pay raises for middle-class teenage children. Would you support that? Of course you wouldn't. But that is precisely what a minimum wage increase would do.

Some readers may object: Why would anyone propose a policy they know would kill jobs and opportunity for the poorest Americans? That doesn't make sense. The answer is that the proponents little worry about destroying those jobs. This is partially due to disagreement on the economics, and partially because they view the safety net as a more than ample substitute for these "dead-end" jobs. Some will get welfare, others will get higher wages— everybody wins!

But conservatives insist this is a terrible defeat for the poor. Pushing people out of work and onto the public dole is never a victory—not for our country, and certainly not for the people themselves. It is unethical to reduce entry-level job opportunities for the poorest Americans just to give a raise to those who are already slightly above them on the economic ladder. It is never right to deny people at the bottom the opportunity to gain the initial work experience they need to become attractive to employers, transition into higher-paying jobs, and build a better future for their families.

I'm going to go out on a limb and guess that many of the people reading this book, like me and my wife, have worked a minimum wage job at some point. What did we get from it? We learned how to show up for work on time, give it our best, get along with others, take directions, and create value with our time and effort. If those lessons were good enough for us, why would we deny them to the poor?

Many years ago, I was sitting on an airplane when a fellow traveler started a conversation. As an economist, I am really interested in what people do all day in their jobs, so I asked him how he made a living. He was the chief financial officer for a company that owns hundreds of fast-food restaurants. I didn't know any-thing about fast food, so I began asking him all sorts of questions about supply chain management and other things that would only interest an economist like me.

But then I made a big mistake. Offhandedly, I asked him, "Do you ever feel bad creating a lot of dead-end jobs?" His face turned a little red and I realized I had screwed up, so I immediately apol-ogized. His response was something I will never forget.

"Let me explain something," he began. "If you work at one of our restaurants and you show up to work and you don't get in a fight or come to work high on drugs, you will probably be pro-moted within a year to assistant manager. You'll be able to support your family. If you work here for four years, and you do a good job, you will be a store manager making a comfortable salary. And if you work hard enough and you get a little lucky and you stick with it, you might even be like me—because I started out flipping burgers on the line."

There are no dead-end jobs in this country. There is dead-end government, perhaps. There is dead-end culture a lot of the time. But there are no dead-end jobs. Remember, conservatives believe that all work is a blessing, whether it makes you rich or not. That is why we recoil at the idea of destroying jobs, moving people onto public assistance, and calling that a victory.

But while minimum wage jobs may have plenty of dignity, it remains true that they sometimes don't pay enough for someone to support a family. This is a real problem in many cases, and we shouldn't pretend it isn't. Conservatives need a solution to that problem that works with markets and for vulnerable people.

Here's one idea: Conservatives can champion an expansion of the Earned Income Tax Credit (EITC). The EITC is a wage subsidy administered through the tax system that has lifted millions of people out of poverty. It rewards work and helps ensure that those at the bottom can take care of their families without living in poverty. Following the eternal principle of free enterprise, people make more when they work more.

The same University of California study that showed how minimum wage hikes reduce employment and income growth at the bottom also found that the EITC had the opposite effect. "[A]nalyses of the EITC," the scholars wrote, "have found it to increase both the employment of low-skilled adults and the incomes available to their families."

The EITC is the most powerful pro-work, antipoverty measure currently in America's economic policy arsenal. But today, the EITC is far more generous to households with children than those without. A childless worker could get about $500 from the EITC in 2014, while a worker with three or more children could get more than $6,000. If we want to create hope for younger workers without children, and help them gain experience to put them on the path to self-reliance, we should expand the EITC to benefit them as well.

We cannot stop there, of course. We must also help create hope for the million-plus Americans facing long-term unemployment. These Americans, who are the worst victims of the Great Recession, are caught in a vicious cycle. The longer they remain unemployed, the harder it is for them to find a job, as their increasingly lengthy jobless spells make them increasingly unattractive to employers.

One reason for chronic unemployment is the mismatch between employees and available jobs. Employers in some places like North Dakota (where unemployment currently sits beneath 3 percent) are desperate for workers, while workers are languishing in places like Atlantic City, New Jersey (11.3 percent unemployment), or Fresno, California (11 percent).[46]

My AEI colleague Michael Strain has suggested creating relocation vouchers for these long-term unemployed. The government could help cover costs for chronically unemployed Americans to move to areas with more plentiful opportunities. Once again, this is an example of government working with labor markets, not against them.

Obviously, not everyone will pick up and move, however generous the subsidy. But at a time when economic conditions vary wildly between regions, the opportunity is a powerful one. Relocation assistance might well offer some the spark they need to begin rebuilding their résumés—and their lives. Further, there is nothing more uniquely American than migration in search of opportunity.

We started out the chapter with the story of Jestina Clayton. Unfortunately, that is not the entrepreneurship story we ordinarily hear from conservative leaders today.

When you listen to conservative politicians on the campaign trail, you'll hear them extolling the virtues of entrepreneurs. But it too often goes something like this: "I met a guy who started off with kind of a rough life in a bad part of town. He didn't have any money; he dropped out of school. But he decided he wanted to open a muffler shop. So he borrowed a little bit of money and the most important thing is he worked hard and day after day, month after month he stuck at it. And now he owns *hundreds* of muffler shops.

"Heck, he's a billionaire!"

That's great. Good for the muffler billionaire. But that's not the primary story we should be telling. Our movement should be focusing not on the people who make it to great wealth, but rather about those who never get rich—but thrive by lifting themselves up out of poverty, building their lives, supporting their families, and understanding their true purpose. That's the essence of American entrepreneurship. Real entrepreneurship is following in the footsteps of Jestina Clayton and approaching your own life as an exciting project, whether you get rich or not.

That is the hope that brought our ancestors to this country. Most immigrants didn't come here with dreams of becoming billionaires. They came here because they did not want to be held down because of where they were born, or their last name, or their religion, or the color of their skin. They wanted to be judged by what they could do with their hard work and merit. They wanted fairness—not redistributive equality, but *real* fairness. Not equality of income, but abundance of opportunity. They just wanted a little conservative social justice.

Conservatives need to be warriors for real fairness, which means we have to fight for real entrepreneurship. We need to fight for the policies and culture that will reverse troubling mobility trends. We need schools that serve children's lives instead of adults' job security. We need to create hope by encouraging job creation for the most marginalized, and declare war on barriers to entrepreneurship at all levels. And we need to revive our moral appreciation for the cultural elements of earned success.

## A HAPPY FIGHT FOR SOCIAL JUSTICE

Our nation has a great deal of need that goes unmet. This is only exacerbated by years of misguided policies and a materialistic culture. The social justice agenda outlined above can restart us on a path toward our best selves and toward our privilege to help the vulnerable.

It is an agenda that promotes values, help, and hope. It means defending a culture of faith, family, community, and work; increasing our charity and protecting the safety net for the truly needy; and fighting for education reform, job creation, and free enterprise as profound moral imperatives. It is an agenda built on a fundamental belief that the best welfare program is a stable family life and a real job.

This agenda will do the most good for the most people—and it will revive the conservative movement. It will allow us to transform the right from a minority that fights against things into a majoritarian social movement that fights for people and champions true social justice with authentically conservative policies.

Fighting for people doesn't mean a massive catalog of new government programs. It does not mean occupying a park and railing against the "1 percent." It means thinking carefully about who is in need and how their need can best be met. In some cases, such as caring for the truly poor, the right solution may well involve the government. In others—such as needy children caught in ineffective schools and entrepreneurs struggling to start businesses—the proper conservative answer is for the government to stop creating harm and get out of the way. In both cases, conservatives can and should be bold warriors for vulnerable people.

Prosperity can grow and more people can have it. We can bring more people out of deprivation, and we have a moral obligation to do it. For too long, we have ceded the notion of compassion and fairness to progressives. But now, we see more and more authentically conservative leaders like Congressman Paul Ryan, Senators Marco Rubio and Mike Lee, former governor Jeb Bush, and many others stepping forward to lead the fight for conservative social justice. They understand that if conservatives become champions of the vulnerable, the spark we set off will relight the fires of hope in a weary country.

In ethical, emotional, and electoral terms, no opportunity could be more promising than this chance to advocate for those who need our help.

# Chapter 6

# FROM PROTEST MOVEMENT TO SOCIAL MOVEMENT:

## A Road Map for the New Right

It was the spark that set off a political insurrection.

On February 19, 2009, a CNBC commentator named Rick Santelli delivered the "rant heard 'round the world" on national television. The country was increasingly on edge as the ravages of the recession were deepening. Banks were going bust. Home values were tanking. Millions of Americans who had taken on mortgages they could not afford were choosing to simply walk away and make their upside-down mortgage someone else's bad investment. And the Obama administration was contemplating ways to provide government-subsidized mortgage relief to everyone.

Reporting live from the floor of the Chicago Mercantile Exchange, Santelli turned to the traders behind him and yelled, "How many of you people want to pay for your neighbors' mortgage that has an extra bathroom and can't pay their bills? Raise their hand! President Obama, are you listening?" He then declared, off the cuff, "We're thinking of having a Chicago Tea Party in July. All you capitalists that want to show up to Lake Michigan, I'm going to start organizing."[1]

With those words, the modern Tea Party was born.

This is how rebellions often get started. Popular frustration builds and builds until someone says or does something that taps into that frustration, setting off a spark that ignites the dry chaff and creates a conflagration. In words commonly attributed to Samuel Adams, the original Tea Party organizer, "It does not require a majority to prevail, but rather an irate, tireless minority keen to set brush fires in people's minds." Scholars dispute whether Adams actually said this, but it certainly captures the spirit of the Tea Parties of both 1773 and 2009.

There was certainly a lot of dry chaff lying around in 2009. Only 20 percent of Americans were satisfied with the way things were going.[2] We had an administration, a government, a ruling elite in Washington that many Americans believed was content with decline. And some activists believed they knew exactly what was causing decline: Politicians of both parties were growing the government grotesquely, spending money we didn't have, bailing out irresponsible bankers and citizens, and unilaterally imposing ruinous taxes and job-killing regulations.

The Tea Party jolted conservative politics. Riding a grassroots wave, Republicans—dominated by Tea Party candidates—took back the House of Representatives in 2010.[3] But the Tea Party had its biggest impact in the states, where conservatives won a higher percentage of seats in state legislatures than at any time in almost a century.

The Tea Party not only took on President Obama and the Democrats; it took on the Republican establishment. Conservative insurgents challenged sitting GOP senators and ran in open primaries against the establishment's handpicked candidates. Some Tea Party candidates ultimately lost general elections that many thought were the GOP's for the taking. But the Tea Party revolt succeeded in electing a host of new conservative reformers—such as Senators Marco Rubio, Mike Lee, and Pat Toomey, among others—who are still making a lasting mark on Washington.

As the Tea Party revolt moved voters at the polls, it also moved ordinary people's minds. According to Gallup, the number of Americans who agreed with the Tea Party that "big government" is the greatest threat to the country rose from 55 percent when President Obama took office to 64 percent in 2011 and reached a record high of 72 by 2013.[4] This was driven mostly by Republicans (92 percent of whom said big government was the nation's greatest threat), but even a majority of Democrats—56 percent—agreed. Never had big government been so discredited in the minds of so many Americans. It looked like a movement that could not be stopped.

But then, in the 2012 election, came a lightning bolt: Barack Obama decisively won reelection over Mitt Romney.

Many conservatives saw this as an unthinkable turn of events just a year before, and pundits debated whether it constituted a repudiation of the Tea Party wave. Indeed, after reaching a high of 32 percent support in November 2010, support for the Tea Party dropped to just 19 percent by November 2014.[5] Was that the beginning of the Tea Party's end? Is the rebellion fated to limp on for a while until it peters out?

It depends. The Tea Party phenomenon is a case study for the conservative movement. As I will show in this chapter, the movement's future relevance depends on whether it can shift from being a protest movement to becoming a social movement.[6] And this holds lessons for the future of conservatism much more broadly.

## HOW TO BUILD A SOCIAL MOVEMENT

A protest movement—a rebellion—is conceptually simple. Identify a source of misery and recruit others to join the fight against it. Whether it's the tyranny of taxation without representation or the effects of an out-of-control government, you identify an enemy and assail it.

Rebellions are inherently oppositional. And oppositions are, by their nature, minorities. With some notable exceptions, such as those where tyrannical racial or religious minorities suppress the population, you don't "rebel" against a minority, but against an unjust majority. Rebellions boil down to us versus them, where "they" are strong and powerful and "we" are weak but courageous.

The key to moving beyond protest and becoming a full social movement is to stop being the opposition and start being the majority. In effect, it is moving from Sam Adams to his cousin John Adams. Or think of it as moving from Boston to Philadelphia. That requires having an intentional design to becoming the majority.

Believe it or not, not everyone wants to be in the majority. Some people prefer to belong to a "remnant," a holdout that bravely carries the truth without compromise in the face of overwhelming opposition. Intellectuals in particular love remnant status, which is why you find such weird causes on college campuses. There is something viscerally satisfying about being part of a minority that is small but right, the sole keepers of special true knowledge. But remnants are rarely responsible for wholesale political change. And since the point of the Tea Party rebellion is to stop the decline of our country, becoming a political remnant simply won't do the trick.

There are four steps to making that transition from minority to majority and turning a protest movement into a broad-based social movement:

1. Launch a rebellion
2. Declare majoritarian values
3. Claim the moral high ground
4. Unite the country behind an agenda

The Tea Party rebellion, and the conservative grassroots it has energized, thus have some choices to make: Does it want to remain at step one, settle for 19 percent support (and falling), and become a permanent political remnant—capable of setting political brushfires, but too weak to bring about real lasting change in our nation? Or does it want to make a run at majority status and build a popular social movement that changes our country forever? Do Tea Party activists want to remain little more than the guardian of fiscally conservative orthodoxy holding the Republican establishment's feet to the fire? Or can the Tea Party become something bigger—a transformational, majoritarian force in American politics that does not simply rebel against American decline, but *reverses* it?

The truth is, if we want to reverse American decline, and not just rail against it, then we do in fact need a conservative majority to prevail. That requires that Tea Party patriots start thinking like a majoritarian social movement.

The good news is the Tea Party has already taken the first step. Now it must take the others. To see how it can, let's look at examples of other rebellions that successfully transitioned into social movements and see what we can learn from their experiences.

## I HAVE A DREAM

The defining social movement of the past half century is the civil rights movement.

The civil rights cause started out in the 1950s as a rebellion against racism. America fought a civil war to end slavery in America. But a century later, slavery had been replaced by institutional racism that was deeply ingrained and relatively uncontroversial in most parts of the country, including in the North. Jim Crow laws and segregation made it harder for African Americans to get a job, obtain education, start businesses, build better lives, and participate fully in American society.

The civil rights movement began with a series of brave, rebellious acts. In 1955, Rosa Parks refused to give up her seat on the bus for a white person, setting off the Montgomery, Alabama, bus boycott. In 1960, black students began a sit-in at a segregated Woolworth's lunch counter in Greensboro, North Carolina, sparking similar sit-ins throughout the South. In 1961, Freedom Riders began riding interstate buses in mixed racial groups to challenge local laws that enforced segregated seating. They were met and beaten by members of the Ku Klux Klan. These and other acts of rebellion captured the nation's attention and set the civil rights movement in motion.

If it had stayed in this initial rebellion phase, the civil rights movement might have burned itself out or become a remnant, like the Black Panther Party or the Nation of Islam. Instead, the leaders of the civil rights movement did something very profound. Rather than continue a perpetual rebellion against an unjust majority, they audaciously claimed that *they* were the ones who possessed majoritarian values.

Dr. Martin Luther King Jr. appealed to the language of our Founding Fathers and challenged Americans by asking why we were not living up to the ideals on which this great nation was founded. Do we not believe that all men are created equal? Don't we hold these ideals sacred? If we do, then that's the majority view. So why aren't we living up to it?

King used his moment in the American spotlight—speaking at the foot of the Lincoln Memorial on August 28, 1963—not to declare unending war on racism, but rather to speak about American values.[7]

*In a sense we've come to our nation's capital to cash a check. When the architects of our republic wrote the magnificent words of the Constitution and the Declaration of Independence, they were signing a promissory note to which every American was to fall heir. This note was a promise that all men, yes, black men as well as white men, would be guaranteed the "unalienable Rights" of "Life, Liberty and the pursuit of Happiness." It is obvious today that America has defaulted on this promissory note, insofar as her citizens of color are concerned. Instead of honoring this sacred obligation, America has given the Negro people a bad check, a check which has come back marked "insufficient funds." But we refuse to believe that the bank of justice is bankrupt. . . .*

*Now is the time to make real the promises of democracy. Now is the time to rise from the dark and desolate valley of segregation to the sunlit path of racial justice. Now is the time to lift our nation from the quicksands of racial injustice to the solid rock of brotherhood. Now is the time to make justice a reality for all of God's children. . . . And so even though we face the difficulties of today and tomorrow, I still have a dream. It is a dream deeply rooted in the American dream. I have a dream that one day this nation will rise up and live*

*out the true meaning of its creed: "We hold these truths to be*
*self-evident, that all men are created equal."*

With these words, the civil rights movement went from rebel-
ling against institutions of racism to claiming majority values.
Civil rights leaders argued that those institutions undercut a
vision of America in which a vast majority of citizens believed.
They were no longer simply saying that racism was unfair to black
people. They were insisting that racism was inconsistent with majoritarian, American founding values.

A key element of majoritarian status is fighting in broad terms
for *people* instead of fighting narrowly against particular evils.
The civil rights movement shifted from fighting *against* racism to
fighting *for* minorities. It fought for their right to vote. It fought
for the right of black kids to attend good schools and get a decent
education. And that pro-people focus attracted a host of allies to
the front lines. In 1964, during the "Freedom Summer," white students from the North came to the South to help register African
Americans to vote and set up "Freedom Schools." The schools
taught subjects that southern public schools refused to cover, such
as black history and constitutional rights.

All this has an immensely important twist. At the time King
was proclaiming that the civil rights movement represented the
values of a sweeping majority, he did not yet have actual majority support. When the March on Washington was held in August
1963, Gallup found that only 23 percent of Americans favored the
march, while 42 percent did not. Even one year after Dr. King delivered his famous speech on the National Mall, just 44 percent
of Americans approved of him.[8] But King continued to speak for
the majority, knowing that over time the majority would come his
way. If you wait to begin speaking for the majority until everyone
agrees, you might not ever get there.

The leaders of the civil rights movement simultaneously took the next step in building a lasting social movement, which is to grab the moral high ground. The values it claimed were not simply majoritarian; they were *transcendentally right*. The problem was not just that bigotry is contrary to our founding principles. Bigotry is *evil*. It is evil now and at all times. This broad moral claim was an appeal to natural law. Civil rights leaders were declaring: Our movement is morally in the right, and those who oppose us are morally in the wrong.

Finally, the civil rights movement began uniting the country behind the new majority. As popular support for the movement steadily grew, Congress passed with overwhelming votes a series of laws—including the Civil Rights Act of 1964 (73–27 in the Senate, 289–126 in the House), the Voting Rights Act of 1965 (79–18 in the Senate, 328–74 in the House), and the Fair Housing Act of 1968 (71–20 in the Senate, 250–172 in the House)—that ended legal discrimination against African Americans. By passing these laws, America was going to be better off because together as a nation, we were finally going to live up to the principles of our founding and our own Declaration of Independence.

In 1969, fully a quarter of Americans said they would not be willing to vote for an African American president. By 1999 the number had shrunk to four percent.[9] And in 2009 the first African American president took the oath of office on the steps of the United States Capitol. Whether you like President Obama or not, we have achieved unity on this question.

Racism has not disappeared, but over time the civil rights movement transformed America. We went from a nation where supporters of civil rights were a minority fighting against powerful institutions to a country where the *opponents* of civil rights were the minority and the political fringe. Civil rights support today is majoritarian, inevitable, and utterly uncontroversial.

## SOBERING UP

The civil rights movement is a profound example of how a rebellion becomes a transformational social movement. But a movement doesn't have to be as world-historical as this. For example, consider Mothers Against Drunk Driving, popularly known by its acronym, MADD.[10]

When I was a kid in the 1970s, drunk driving was considered to be no big deal. You didn't want to get caught doing it, but the worst part was crashing your dad's car or running over your neighbor's mailbox. Drunk driving didn't make you a pariah. It was how some people routinely got home from parties.

Then, on May 3, 1980, all that began to change. Candace Lightner's 13-year-old daughter, Cari, was walking to a church carnival in Fair Oaks, California, when she was killed by a hit-and-run driver.[11] When police called Candace to tell her they had the driver in custody, they failed to even mention that he had been drunk behind the wheel. It wasn't important enough to bring up. Only after Candace drove by the spot where her daughter had been killed and stopped to talk to some officers did she learn the truth. The driver was out on bail from another drunk driving hit-and-run. It was his fifth offense in four years.

Outraged, Candace began researching the issue. She discovered that alcohol was involved in nearly 60 percent of fatal car crashes. Thousands of kids were dying at the hands of drunk drivers. Something had to be done. So together with her friend Sue LeBrun-Green she started Mothers Against Drunk Driving. Cari's still-decorated bedroom served as the organization's first office.[12]

MADD began as a rebellion against the social attitude that condoned a dangerous activity while it was claiming lives. It could have easily ended there. After all, that's what happened to many other, similar parental rebellions. Do you remember the 1980s movement to curb sexually explicit and violent lyrics in music? Probably not. This movement was spearheaded by Al Gore's then wife, Tipper Gore. The group she founded, the Parents Music Resource Center (PMRC), got attention for a while. It elicited brief pushback from some players in the music industry. Frank Zappa, my favorite rock star as a kid, testified against music labeling and called it an un-American form of censorship. Numerous artists released songs and albums mocking Gore and her labeling effort. The PMRC rebellion soon fizzled out. It had little lasting impact— as any parent can tell you who still has to quickly change the station while driving with his or her children.

MADD, on the other hand, did not fizzle out. It became a mass social movement that changed America forever. So what did MADD do differently?

After its initial rebellion, MADD deliberately claimed majoritarian values. Every parent in America wants to protect her children from danger. Keeping kids safe is a majoritarian value. Mothers Against Drunk Driving challenged the country by saying: "When we don't take this problem seriously, we are not keeping our kids safe. That is contrary to what all of us agree are our priorities."

Like a true majority, MADD went from fighting against drunk drivers to fighting for children. Its rhetoric and its proposals all focused on protecting innocent victims. Consider how it led to the National Minimum Drinking Age Act, a bill that reduced a state's share of federal highway dollars if it failed to raise the drinking age to twenty-one. President Reagan was listening to objections that it violated his support for states' rights. But then he asked, "Well, wait a minute. Doesn't this help save kids' lives?" His transportation secretary told him it did. "Well, then I support it," Reagan told her.[13] MADD had won over the president of the United States by fighting for kids. At a Rose Garden ceremony on

July 17, 1984, Reagan signed the bill into law. Candace Lightner pinned a "MADD" button on his lapel.

MADD wasn't done yet. In the years that followed, it got states to increase penalties for driving under the influence. It pressed state legislatures to pass laws reducing the legal blood alcohol limit—always on behalf of kids, as the majority of Americans would want. It successfully lobbied states across the country to enact and enforce seat belt laws. It pressed communities across the country to institute public sobriety checkpoints.

MADD successfully claimed the moral high ground. Drunk driving kills kids. Therefore, drunk driving isn't just unfortunate, it's morally wrong. We take it for granted today, but MADD transformed America's view of drunk driving. The same nation that once saw drunk drivers as mildly foolish now viewed them as people who did something bad, and viewed people who did it repeatedly as personally immoral. We want them locked up.

Finally, MADD united the country behind its crusade. By 1994, MADD was the most popular charity in America.[14] Celebrities and politicians jostled to be publicly associated with such a noble cause. Want to see unity? Get twenty people who agree on nothing else into a room, and ask how many think the penalties for drunk driving are too lax.

Reflect for a moment on this remarkable trajectory. First, MADD rebelled against a culture that turned a blind eye to drunk driving. Second, it identified the perpetrators as a minority who were trampling all over the values of a silent majority. Third, it claimed the moral high ground by insisting drunk driving was not foolish but rather ethically wrong and shifted from fighting against villains to championing kids. And finally, after passing a series of measures to penalize and discourage drunk driving, MADD united the country behind the new majoritarian view and turned its immediate momentum into enduring cultural change.

This is how a rebellion becomes a social movement.

## THE NEXT STEP FOR THE TEA PARTY

The Tea Party needs to replicate this process. And now we hold in our hands the blueprint. Tea Partiers need to follow the same steps as the civil rights movement, MADD, and the many other social movements, large and small, that started out as impassioned protests.

It has already accomplished the first step—sparking a popular rebellion. The Tea Party tapped into the frustrations of millions of ordinary Americans, inspiring many to get involved politically, brush up on the U.S. Constitution, and organize demonstrations. It enlisted the activism or sympathy of nearly one in five Americans for this protest. It restored a focus on fiscal discipline on Capitol Hill, ended the practice of special interest earmarks, and stiffened the spines of the GOP establishment. Now the Tea Party has to go after the persuadable majority, who, polls show, remain open to its message.

That's why stage two is proclaiming majoritarian values. Today, everyone knows what the Tea Party is against—big government, taxes, regulation, spending, deficits, debt, and Obamacare. But only minority movements define themselves by what they're against. Majorities define themselves by the values and people they are for. What is the Tea Party for? What is its moral purpose? What is its governing agenda?

The Tea Party must dedicate itself to the positive fruits of its principles. The power of free enterprise will help Americans escape poverty and dependency by creating good-paying jobs, restoring upward mobility, and creating a new culture of opportunity. Work, mobility, and opportunity are majoritarian values. These are the values that animate the conservative heart. The Tea Party can show the conservative heart to America.

Americans need to see the Tea Party as the vanguard of a new right that fights for the whole country. The grass roots should consider themselves heroes on behalf of those left behind in the Obama economy—whether they support Tea Party leaders or not. The conservative social movement can't dismiss as moochers people who can't find jobs and have to take government help. On the contrary, these are precisely the people who need our help. It isn't ordinary citizens who are to blame, but the architects of disastrous economic policies that have destroyed opportunities for independence. The Tea Party can fight for all the people in this country.

The third step is to seize the moral high ground in this fight by asserting moral rightness. It is not an economic error but a moral failure that so many Americans have been marginalized and left behind. As we have discussed already, the two moral imperatives that illuminate this are fairness and compassion. It is neither fair nor compassionate to content ourselves with an economic recovery that only accrues to top earners. It is neither fair nor compassionate to threaten the solvency of the core safety net by extending it boundlessly upward into the middle class. And it is neither fair nor compassionate to saddle future generations with ruinous debt. *Fairness* and *compassion* are the words that should appear in every speech and article.

And finally, the Tea Party needs to unite the country around a vision for a better America. That requires storytelling. Tea Partiers need to craft an optimistic vision of what a better America looks like ten years from now. We envision an America that is rising, in which everyone can earn their success, and where government empowers rather than restrains people who seek to strike out on their own.

Imagine an America where a kid graduating from high school who does not go on to college does not face a life of unemployment and social assistance. Instead, he has his choice of jobs where he can align his skills with his talents—whether he gets rich or not—and earn his success on the basis of hard work and personal responsibility. Imagine an America where struggling people's prospects of escaping poverty through work are better than they are today. Imagine a country where the safety net is solid, secure, and used sparingly—only by those who are truly indigent, and always with work requirements in place.

Imagine an America that is a beacon of hope for the world, a place to which every immigrant from all around the world wants to come. Imagine an America that can truly lift up the world—whether through the force of our example, trade, diplomacy, or even military might when necessary.

When the Tea Party unites the country behind this kind of moral, majoritarian vision and fights to make it a reality for everyone, it will cease to be a conservative rebellion. It will become the new moral majority.

## FIGHTING FOR PEOPLE

At this point, some conservative readers might feel skeptical. Am I saying we should abandon our objections to Obamacare, excessive spending, and debt?

Not at all. I'm simply asking you to remember *why* Tea Party conservatives oppose Obamacare. We dislike the health law because Obamacare is hurting *people*. It has caused millions to lose their doctors and their health plans. By shifting employers' incentives, it is stripping valuable work hours away from people who are already underemployed. It is raising the premiums and deductibles of people who cannot afford to pay more.

This is not to say America doesn't need health-care reform—God knows we do, and conservatives believe in finding ways to expand access to health care for people who do not have it. But Obamacare is the wrong way, and we have better solutions—from Health Savings Accounts to association health plans that allow small businesses to band together and negotiate the same kinds of discounts big corporations do. Yes, we need to repeal Obamacare, but Americans also need to see us championing conservative reforms like these that will improve people's lives.

The same goes for spending and debt. We are against growing the national debt not because ordinary Americans care about negative fiscal balances, but because irresponsibility hurts real people. As we saw in detail in the last chapter, we need only look to Europe for a prime example of how unsustainable debt leads to insolvency, and how insolvency yields austerity cuts that fall the hardest on vulnerable people. Anyone who believes in a social safety net for the truly indigent must demand that we avoid austerity by reining in spending in a thoughtful way while we can easily do so. If you love the poor, you must be a fiscal conservative. There's no other way.

The same goes for education. Why do we want education reform? It's not because we hate teachers' unions. It's because we *love kids*. It's because the abuses of the bureaucracies and unions are eating up all of the public school money while resisting accountability and innovation, which hurts kids—especially poor kids. We believe in school choice because it will unleash innovation and allow poor families to escape failing schools. We believe in collective bargaining reform because it frees school districts from the stranglehold of collective bargaining rules—allowing them to save money, add more teachers, and hire and fire based on merit instead of seniority. It is common decency to put the interests of children ahead of the interests of employees.

Making the transition from a rebellion to a social movement does not mean we cease opposition to bad things. It means that we stop leading with what we are against. We lead with the people we are fighting for.

This is something our Founding Fathers understood. When Samuel Adams and the rest of our founding generation made the transition from rebellion to social movement, they had a long list of grievances. The bulk of the Declaration of Independence— about 65 percent of it—is actually a bill of attainder against King George III, detailing his "history of repeated injuries and usurpations, all having in direct object the establishment of an absolute Tyranny over these States."

But that bill of attainder is not what our Founding Fathers led with when they wrote the Declaration. They led with an appeal to "the Laws of Nature and of Nature's God." They opened with an audacious, universal moral claim: "We hold these truths to be self-evident, that all men are created equal, that they are endowed by their Creator with certain unalienable Rights, that among these are Life, Liberty and the pursuit of Happiness. That to secure these rights, Governments are instituted among Men, deriving their just powers from the consent of the governed." Talk about fighting for people!

Everything in the first two paragraphs of the Declaration of Independence is a claim to majority values. "All men are created equal" is a majoritarian statement. Our Founders were declaring that independence was inevitable, that they were the majority, and anyone whose eyes were open would think like them.

They took the moral high ground. They were not declaring independence on their own authority, just to stick a thorn in the monarch's side. They were doing so because that's what the moral law of "Nature's God" demanded. They were doing so because our "Creator" has endowed all men with unalienable rights. This was a deeply reverential claim. When people believed that God Himself wanted the colonies to be free of King George, King George had a big problem on his hands.

There was no appeal to economic efficiency in their argument at all. In May 1776, just a few weeks before they met in Philadelphia, George Mason had written the Virginia Declaration of Rights. In it, he announced that all men have inherent rights to "the enjoyment of life and liberty, with the means of acquiring and possessing property, and pursuing and obtaining happiness and safety." Thomas Jefferson deliberately dropped "property" and "safety" in favor of "the pursuit of happiness." He knew he could not take the moral high ground with materialistic arguments. The pursuit of property was an economic claim. The pursuit of happiness was a moral statement. Moreover, happiness is ineluctably personal. It is something each person defines for him or herself. In short, it is a promise that each of us should have the freedom to determine our own ends.

By the way, just as with Martin Luther King, it was not clear that the Constitution's Framers constituted an actual majority when they adopted their majoritarian outlook. According to historian Robert Calhoon, "The patriots received active support from perhaps 40 to 45 percent of the white populace, and at most no more than a bare majority." Another 15 to 20 percent were loyalists, and the rest "tried to avoid involvement in the struggle—some of them deliberate pacifists, others recent immigrants, and many more simple apolitical folk."[15]

After all we grew up hearing and reading, it's hard to imagine Americans not knowing or caring about the revolution. But it makes sense. As it happens, my grandfather's grandfather's grandfather, John Brooks, married his wife, Abigail Richardson, on the Fourth of July, 1776, in Boston. There is zero evidence that they knew or cared a whit about what was going on in Philadelphia that very day.

Only after Jefferson had claimed majoritarian values and staked a moral claim to independence—then and only then—did his Declaration finally offer the "what" of the revolution. That was the list of charges against George III. That bill of attainder was important in its time but retains little meaning today. What is transcendent, what is permanent, is not the "what" of the American Revolution but the "why." It is the declaration of the inalienable rights that our children still memorize to this day. That is what endures. That is what transformed a tax revolt into a social movement—the social movement that is still the United States of America.

If decades from now people won't remember the Tea Party's grievances with President Obama, that will actually be a signal of our success. If the Tea Party succeeds, it will be because the "why" of the movement—who we fought for, not what or who we fought against—has endured.

The Boston Tea Party took place on December 16, 1773. The Declaration of Independence was signed on July 4, 1776. There is a reason why we celebrate the "Spirit of '76" not the "Spirit of '73." To be sure, the American Revolution could not have happened without the antitax revolt that began in Boston Harbor that day. But we take a day off each year to celebrate the social movement that began in Independence Hall three years later. That is what transformed our nation and the world. That is what should serve as the model for the conservative movement today.

But if we are to transform the Tea Party revolt into a majoritarian social movement that changes America forever, we need to learn to talk differently. We need to find ways to open the hearts and minds of the persuadable majority. We need to adopt the language of compassion and fairness, and show Americans that conservatives are happy warriors with a moral mission—to fight for the people who need us most, whether they vote for us or not.

How to do that is the subject of the next chapter.

# Chapter 7

# THE SEVEN HABITS OF HIGHLY EFFECTIVE CONSERVATIVES:

## How to Talk So Americans Will Listen

I t's time to return to the brutal truth that motivated this whole book: Conservatives have the right stuff to lift up the poor and vulnerable—but have been generally terrible at winning people's hearts.

We are the fiscally responsible grown-ups, the stern authority figures, the ones the people usually trust to run a tight economic ship. But that is not primarily what the country wants. Voters want leaders who care about people like them. They yearn for leaders who feel their pain and respond in tangible ways. And that has just not been us.

Some think that responsible voters should be less emotional and more logical. I myself have wished this sometimes. But the truth is, deep down we all know that we wouldn't vote for someone who doesn't care about us, and even less for someone who doesn't even like us.

Over the past five years, I have asked hundreds of conservatives a simple question: *What is the biggest thing that bothers you about President Obama?* And I started to notice a trend. Conservatives start by naming some specific policy complaint—their opposition to Obamacare or to his foreign policies. But these responses never quite ring complete. Of course conservatives disagree with President Obama on policy grounds. But that is true for virtually every progressive politician, and many of them receive more grudging respect from conservatives—think Bill Clinton—than President Obama does.

It's clear these substantive disagreements are only scratching the surface. Everyone can sense that a deeper, latent problem lies beneath them. Some pundits try to slander half the country by calling that latent force racism. This is unfounded, as studies showing equal conservative support for black and white conservative candidates make clear.[1]

Here is what *really* bugs conservatives about the president: He acts like he has utter contempt for us and the values we hold dear.

Remember how the president characterized conservative values to an audience of Democratic donors in 2012? "If you get sick, you're on your own. If you can't afford college, you're on your own. If you don't like that some corporation is polluting your air or the air that your child breathes, then you're on your own." This isn't meaningful policy discourse or respectful political disagreement. The most powerful man in the world told an audience that *you*, if you are a conservative American, are a selfish person.[2]

Or remember, back in 2008, when then candidate Obama offered his theory of why some working-class voters lean Republican. "They get bitter," he explained, and "they cling to guns or religion or antipathy to people who aren't like them or anti-immigrant sentiment or anti-trade sentiment as a way to explain their frustrations."[3] If you are a heartland conservative, the future president implied that you are a bigot and a rube.

President Obama says one contemptuous thing after another about us and our deepest-held values, slurs we know to be untrue but which go largely unanswered because he's the president of the United States.

It feels lousy, doesn't it?

Now turn this feeling around. Let's put ourselves in the shoes of Americans who are basically apolitical, trying to make a living since the Great Recession and really struggling to get by. There are millions and millions of Americans who fit this description. Too often, these Americans hear Republican politicians talk about those on welfare as being lazy and preferring not to work. When they hear this, are people likely to say that conservatives truly care about people like them? Or are they more likely to perceive in conservatives the same kind of poorly concealed contempt that President Obama has for *us*?

The answer requires no conjecture, because we have evidence: Ordinary Americans believe conservatives don't care about them, let alone about people who are even poorer or more vulnerable. Conservatives are perceived as aligning moral worth with wealth. Innumerable polls outline this reality. One, in 2013, found that Americans are *five times* more likely to say the Republican Party is not compassionate as they are to say it is compassionate.[4]

That's bad news. And it gets even worse. In what seems like a political version of Stockholm syndrome, even most conservatives say they agree with that negative assessment of themselves. An amazing study from the University of California, Los Angeles, showed that conservative heartlessness is basically an "inaccurate stereotype": In practice, conservatives were just as generous as liberals when it came to helping those down on their luck through no fault of their own. Yet the study found that even a majority of *conservative* citizens bought into the myth nonetheless![5] Both liberals and conservatives predicted conservatives would be less generous than they actually were.

I can relate to this confusion. Back in my teaching days, I specialized in the economics of charitable giving. I was pretty excited when I realized that hardly any research at all had compared charitable giving by conservatives and liberals, and I took up the task myself. Despite being a conservative, my expectation was that liberals certainly give more than conservatives. But the data got in the way of that assumption, as I have already shown you. Conservatives give more to charity than liberals, despite having less income, on average.

The data make it especially ironic that most Americans—including most conservative Americans—believe the "conservative heart" is an oxymoron. Nearly everyone, no matter how they vote, has bought into this delusional caricature of right-wing cruelty. Forget the merits of conservative policy solutions, whether they're targeted at the disappearance of work or the failures of the War on Poverty. Americans don't trust us to address these challenges because they do not think we are fundamentally caring people.

Why do so many people share the same false impression?

Many conservatives will complain that we don't get a fair shake in the mainstream media. That is certainly true as far as it goes. But consider that today, this media monopoly is arguably *less* of a problem than it was in the past. Thanks to talk radio, cable news, and the Internet, conservative media have proliferated. So why hasn't our public image improved accordingly?

Others will say the problem is liberal politicians. They score points by misrepresenting our message to struggling Americans. Sure enough, as we just saw, the president never seems to miss an opportunity to tear down his political foes and portray ordinary conservatives in the harshest possible light. Is this bad leadership? Sure. But is this a new or exceptional practice? Not even close. It's called basic power politics. The insults per se aren't the problem. If a voter trusted a conservative's heart, he or she wouldn't take them seriously. If the soil weren't already fertile, the seeds of resentment would never take root.

Forget the scapegoats. When the vast majority of Americans agree that conservatives are not compassionate, the time has come for a little introspection. The central problem is not what others say about us. It is what *we* say about *ourselves*. Conservatives have struggled to talk about our own values in a way that connects with Americans. Our solutions to the great moral and practical challenges of our time fall on deaf ears because we fail to achieve credibility.

One of the things that I am privileged to do as part of my work at AEI is to speak regularly with politicians, policymakers, and candidates about ways to communicate our ideas more effectively. As I described earlier, we hold regular debate training and messaging seminars for members of Congress where we discuss how conservatives—or anyone, for that matter—can open hearts and minds so that Americans will listen to us and trust us to solve the deep problems facing our country. In this chapter, I will share with you the same seven lessons I cover with members of Congress.

1. Be a moralist.
2. Fight for people, not against things.
3. Get happy.
4. Steal all the best arguments.
5. Go where you're not welcome.
6. Say it in thirty seconds.
7. Break your bad habits.

## 1. BE A MORALIST.

My AEI colleague Jonah Goldberg recently wrote a book entitled *The Tyranny of Clichés*. One of the clichés is that conservatives are rigid, judgmental ideologues. Progressives, by contrast, are praised as flexible pragmatists who seek practical solutions and go wherever the data lead them.

Year after year, this tired, old narrative yields an equally tired piece of advice: *If conservatives want to win again, they need to forget the moralizing and deal only with facts and figures.*

This is a misunderstanding. Conservatives are not too moralistic—they are not moralistic enough! When it comes to the kitchen-table policy issues that affect most American families, progressives make bold proclamations about fairness and social justice that sail by, virtually unquestioned. Conservatives, on the other hand, come across as wonky, unfeeling materialists whose primary focus is money. The left talks about the human experience while the right talks about GDP growth, tax rates, and spending levels.

This is one of the greatest political ironies of our time: In fact, it is materialistic to presume that money and the redistribution of wealth alone can solve tangled social problems. It is materialistic to conflate human dignity with one's position on the income scale, and to assert that anyone is oppressed if others earn more than they do. But when progressives present their views to the American people, they often wrap these fundamentally materialistic premises in richly moral language. And voters reward them for it.

Conversely, deep down, conservatives tend to be moralists. Conservatism at its best is a series of courageous—and, frankly, subversive—moral assertions about what it means to be human. We assert that there is great raw material in every single person, regardless of their circumstances. This is a revolutionary stance! We assert that providing pathways to work and holding people to high moral standards are not acts of condescension, but of brotherly love. We assert that the deep principles of justice require far more of us than simply rejiggering the distribution of wealth.

Yet when we make our case to the American people, we usually wrap these noble concepts in the hideous packaging of materialism. When we cheerlead entrepreneurship, for example, we usually heap praise on rags-to-riches outliers who are now multinational executives. Seldom do we explain that the entrepreneurial spirit is priceless because it captures the American spirit in each of our lives. We're moralists trapped in a materialistic vocabulary. We forfeit our best territory the instant the debate begins.

As a tangible example, take the seemingly interminable debates over minimum wage. Raising the minimum wage is a surprisingly bad instrument for achieving a worthy goal—namely, boosting the incomes of working Americans. Using the force of law to make vulnerable people artificially expensive to employ destroys job opportunities for the people who need them most urgently. Compared to more effective policies that could actually achieve the same desired end, minimum wage hikes hurt the working poor whom they are meant to assist.

But that's not exactly how this argument plays out in Washington.

Right out of the gate, progressives speak in moral terms. "Come on, it's just a little bit more money. Why don't you love poor people? You don't think the billionaires who own Wal-Mart can afford to pay a few more dollars per hour?"

The conservative response almost always takes the form of an economics lecture. "Whether Wal-Mart can afford three bucks more is not the point. Raising the minimum wage increases the cost of labor. If you raise the cost of labor, businesses will respond by using less of it. Firms only create jobs when adding marginal workers will generate net revenue. So if you raise the minimum wage, you are pricing cheap labor out of the market. QED!"

One of these two people sounds like they have workers' best interests in their hearts. The other comes across like a mildly sociopathic economist. Instead of championing low-wage Americans, conservatives sound like tax accountants to billionaires. It's not that the conservative's economic case is wrong. It isn't. But it cannot be the only, or even the primary, tool in our arsenal. When it is, our very rhetoric seems to prove the accusation that conservatives elevate economics above the human heart.

Americans are not materialists. Most find materialism noxious and ugly, as they should. They are uneasy at its presence in their own lives and they rebel against it in public life. So when conservatives present the policies America needs with materialistic language, we are placing our ideas in a box so unattractive that people simply don't want to look inside. They instinctively side with moral over materialistic rhetoric, and often vote for progressive politicians as a result. But, I have argued, many of the policies they subsequently get are materialistic to the core. The people are left dissatisfied and convinced that both sides are awful.

In theory, there are two ways politicians could right the ship. The left could *become* less materialistic or the right could *sound* less materialistic. In my view, Americans deserve both these developments. Politics ought to be a virtuous and tireless competition for the moral high ground. But since this book is intended to celebrate and improve conservatism, let's focus on the second task.

Center-right leaders didn't always speak like economics professors. This trend largely started as a by-product of the conservative economics revolution of the 1970s. Before Ronald Reagan, as crazy as it sounds, you could actually be a high-level politician in America and not understand the basic laws of supply and demand. That's how we got draconian wage and price controls under a Republican president, Richard Nixon, and the outbreak of shortages that they generated.

If you were alive in the 1970s, you remember this nightmare. When OPEC imposed an oil embargo on the United States, our self-imposed price controls meant everyone had to wait in line for fuel. I remember sitting in the backseat of my dad's Plymouth Valiant in 1973, stuck in an endless line at the gas station. It was a Republican president who distorted markets, wasted millions of hours of Americans' time, and led to the first time I ever heard my poor, sweet dad let fly a cuss word. (As a child, that last offense seemed like sufficient justification for Nixon's impeachment.)

But while Nixon was busy ordering "a freeze on all prices and wages throughout the United States," conservative intellectuals were hard at work on a very different approach. Institutions like the American Enterprise Institute and the *Wall Street Journal* editorial page gave birth to supply-side economics. It was a new school of thought based on the simple premise that people respond to incentives. If you make something more attractive, like work or savings, people will do more of it. And if you make something less attractive by punishing it with high tax rates, they will do relatively less of it.

In September 1974, an up-and-coming economist named Arthur Laffer sat down for drinks at the Hotel Washington with President Gerald Ford's chief of staff and his deputy. You might have heard of these men: Their names were Don Rumsfeld and Dick Cheney. Laffer wanted to explain why Ford's plan to impose a 5 percent tax surcharge was a bad idea. He grabbed a cloth napkin, pulled out a pen, and sketched a doodle that became known as the "Laffer Curve." (Who writes on a cloth napkin, by the way?) It showed that when taxes are higher than a certain point, raising rates will lower revenues because people will work and earn less.[6]

This insight helped launch the Reagan Revolution in the 1980s. It produced what was then the longest peacetime economic expansion in history. But it also sparked a new crusade on the political right to raise America's economic literacy. People started thinking, If we can explain tax incentives with a napkin doodle, we can explain economics to everyone! Like a college sophomore home for Christmas break, Republicans became earnest explainers who would corner everyone in earshot to explain what they'd learned. To win forever, it seemed, all conservatives had to do was keep repeating that reducing marginal tax rates increases the incentive to work and stimulates growth!

This quickly turned into myopia. Republican politicians started fixating on economic expansion as an end in itself. They spoke as if growth were all that mattered, ignoring the deeper reason we care about growth in the first place—it gives more people a better shot to build their own lives. Over time, these hopeful, optimistic foot soldiers in Reagan's revolution started focusing less on the positive things Reagan fought for and more on the things he opposed—like high taxes, high spending, regulations, and debt. And what is the result? Conservatives stopped winning. Taxes are rising, spending is higher, regulations are growing, and our debt is skyrocketing. Meanwhile, Republicans have created a reputation for themselves as being a party of heartless Scrooges.

It's time to reverse that mistake. Let's return to the minimum wage debate. Stop laboring to explain inflation cycles, consumption patterns, and the laws of supply and demand. Lead with your heart and offer a statement of principle.

"I believe that in America, if you work hard and play by the rules, our society should make sure you can support yourself and your family." Now people are listening to you.

Next, pose a question. "So, what is the best way to make work pay for folks toward the bottom of the economic ladder?"

State that minimum wage hikes would actually set back that goal. "Increasing the minimum wage would give some people raises, but many of the most vulnerable would lose their jobs! We need to fight for those people."

Finally, step up with a superior alternative. For example, "I have a better way to make work pay. Instead of raising the minimum wage, we should expand the Earned Income Tax Credit. This supplements poor people's paychecks without destroying their jobs. Poor Americans need and deserve this."

This is a bit harder than blithely saying demagogic nonsense like, "Let's give America a raise!" But if you master it, look at what you've accomplished. This little monologue combines several of the tactics I'm about to describe, but it all started when you began with a statement of moral purpose. From the very beginning, your audience is not thinking that you seem heartless. They have the accurate impression that you genuinely care, and they're willing to listen to the rest.

This is a useful habit for all of us, even if we never set foot on a debate stage. The next time you are about to have an argument with your spouse, don't launch right in. Start with a statement of moral purpose: "Honey, first of all, I want you to remember how much I love you. I know you want to do what's best for our family."

Instantly, that becomes a totally different conversation. Okay, your spouse might also think you need to see a psychiatrist. But you get the idea.

No matter the topic, never start with *what* you want to talk about. Start with *why*. If you lead with your heart, you'll have a shot at winning over everybody within earshot. Their hearts will open in response. So practice your pitch—and make it a statement of moral purpose.

## 2. FIGHT FOR PEOPLE, NOT AGAINST THINGS.

I have known former House Speaker Newt Gingrich for many years. He is unfailingly quirky and interesting, and many of his ideas have proved visionary. Newt came to national prominence as the architect of the "Republican revolution" of 1994, the midterm election when House Republicans won a majority for the first time in decades.

I used to teach courses in management and leadership, and now I live those subjects every day at the helm of AEI. So it probably will not surprise you that I harbor a long-standing fascination with seeking out the best leadership practices. Figuring there was nobody better to ask about herding cats in Washington, D.C., than Speaker Gingrich, I asked him what was the biggest challenge he faced as the new Speaker of the House.

He didn't respond, "The press." Nor did he reply, "A recalcitrant president from the opposite party." No—Newt's biggest challenge was his own Republican members. Not their character or their principles, but their mindset. Winning a majority and actually operating like a majority turned out to be very different things. Even though the numbers now said otherwise, Republicans were still thinking like the minority.

As I explained in the last chapter, in a democratic system, the minority is by definition the opposition. Their de facto position is fighting against the ideas of the other side. Political minorities fight against something that's more powerful than they are. And over time, their entire self-identity can become utterly reliant on acting like the principled underdog.

When conservatives fight against teachers' unions, fight against Obamacare, fight against debt, spending, the expansion of government, we are not setting an agenda. We are reacting to an agenda. When this process is iterated over and over, conservatives start to forget that fighting against things is not our true goal, but merely one tactic for reaching larger goals. We let our temporary political fortunes ossify into a permanent minoritarian mindset.

This is an error. First of all, conservatives are not actually in the minority. According to Gallup, significantly more Americans identify as conservative (38 percent) than as moderate (34 percent) or liberal (24 percent).[8] Liberals are the smallest ideological minority, yet they adroitly think and act like a majority. They claim incessantly that they're fighting for the "99 percent." That is inherently majoritarian language, and the public frequently rewards them with legislative majorities to match it. Paradoxically, though conservatives outnumber liberals, we have become accustomed to behaving like a minority and fighting against things.

Let's return to the 1980s for a moment. Conservatives constantly invoke the memory of Ronald Reagan, an excellent president. Was it Reagan who led the conservative movement to fight against things?

The answer is no. On the contrary, Reagan understood better than anyone that a minority fights against things while a majority fights for people. He understood the dangers of limitless government, to be sure. But he always brought the conversation home to the people hurt by overreach. He didn't pretend that most people regard the size of the government as an intrinsic philosophical evil.

Here are President Reagan's own words, delivered at the 1980 Republican National Convention in Detroit as he made the case for his election:

*Together, let us make this a new beginning. Let us make a commitment to care for the needy; to teach our children the values and the virtues handed down to us by our families. . . .*

*Ours are not problems of abstract economic theory. [They]*

*are problems of flesh and blood; problems that cause pain and destroy the moral fiber of real people who should not suffer the further indignity of being told by the government that it is all somehow their fault.*

*Work and family are at the center of our lives, the foundation of our dignity as a free people. When we deprive people of what they have earned, or take away their jobs, we destroy their dignity and undermine their families. . . . We have to move ahead, but we're not going to leave anyone behind. Thanks to the economic policies of the Democratic Party, millions of Americans find themselves out of work. Millions more have never even had a fair chance to learn new skills, hold a decent job, or secure for themselves and their families a share in the prosperity of this nation. It is time to put America back to work; to make our cities and towns resound with the confident voices of men and women of all races, nationalities, and faiths bringing home to their families a decent paycheck they can cash for honest money.*

*For those without skills, we'll find a way to help them get skills. For those without job opportunities, we'll stimulate new opportunities, particularly in the inner cities where they live. For those who have abandoned hope, we'll restore hope and we'll welcome them into a great national crusade to make America great again!*

Notice how different this sounds from many of today's angriest voices who scramble to claim Reagan's mantle. His speech is strikingly positive in tenor. It is optimistic, aspirational, and resoundingly pro-people.

Take a look at this "word cloud" of Reagan's speech. The more frequently a word is used, the larger it appears. What single word stands out the most?

True, "government" shows up with prominence. That is to be expected in any policy speech. But "people" is Reagan's most frequently repeated word. He mentions "people" 38 times in his speech. In fact, when you add in all the other times he talks about the *kinds* of people he is fighting for—"families," "children," "the needy," "the elderly," "immigrants," "workers," and so on—the number rises to 87.

Spending was mentioned just four times, "deficit" just twice, and "regulation" twice. Zero mentions of "debt." The only specific policy words even visible are "tax" (17 mentions) and "economic" (18).

When Ronald Reagan made his case to the American people, he didn't spend a lot of time talking about what he was fighting against. He spent most of his speech talking about who he was fighting for. This is what conservatives too often forget. We spend much too much time explaining economic policy to people who just want to hear how we can improve their lives and the lives of the poor.

Even when economics is not used to fight against things, explaining it generally distracts from our first-order goal. Economics runs quietly in the background, like your computer's operating system. This is certainly important: You need to get it right or you're in trouble.

But Republicans today have become like a bunch of computer

geeks talking about "bits," "algorithms," and "binary values." Most people don't understand that stuff or much care about it. A hardworking parent isn't interested in soldering. They just want their phones to work.

Even real-life engineers know this, by the way. When Apple advertises their new devices, they don't do it by extolling their great chips or processing speeds, or talking about the engineering problems they faced. Instead, they show all the amazing things people can do with the device. They illustrate in vivid colors how owning Apple products will make your life better. Conservative communicators need to take the hint. We should stop selling chips and processors and start selling better lives.[9]

This lesson was a difficult pill for me to swallow. I have a PhD in public policy. I'm the president of a *think tank*. I love to debunk myths with data and technical arguments. One of my favorite things to do on weekends is lean back in a comfy chair with a good academic study. My colleagues and I can and do spend hours carefully measuring the pros and cons of particular public policy proposals.

So if I can train myself to swap negative, technical arguments against things in exchange for positive arguments on behalf of people, anyone can.

## 3. GET HAPPY.

Andrew Luck is one of the most successful quarterbacks in the National Football League. In his first three seasons, he led his team to two division titles, including the second-biggest playoff comeback in NFL history.

But the Indianapolis Colts star has become known for more than the cannon attached to his shoulder. According to the *Wall*

*Street Journal*, "Luck has become famous for congratulating—sincerely and enthusiastically—any player to hit him hard." The *Journal* contacted a dozen players who recently had hit or sacked Luck, and they all told the same story. "Any sack is met with a hearty congratulations, such as 'great job' or 'what a hit!' He yells it after hard hits that don't result in sacks, too. It is, players say, just about the weirdest thing any quarterback does in the NFL." [10]

Once, Washington Redskins linebacker Ryan Kerrigan hit Luck so hard that the quarterback fumbled the football. Since he was scrambling to retrieve it, he could not offer his customary congratulations. But don't worry—Luck sought him out later in the game and told him what a great job he was doing. Kerrigan was baffled. "You want to say thank you," he explained, "but then you say 'wait a second—I'm not supposed to like you!'"

Andrew Luck is both unusually aggressive and preternaturally cheerful. His good humor is genuine, but it has the added effect of throwing the opposing team off balance. They don't know what to make of him. Virtue, it turns out, is a competitive advantage.

I have no idea if Andrew Luck is a conservative. But conservatives need to be more like Andrew Luck.

As a quick detour into neuroscience will soon show us, it is extremely challenging to overcome a bad first impression. And yes, there is a lot to be angry about in America today. Conservatives worry the country we love is in decline. We're mad about it. But the plain fact is that debating with anger turns people off. The public is instinctively attracted to happy warriors who fight in a spirit of charity.

This is another classic Reagan lesson that some modern conservatives misunderstand. How often did you see Ronald Reagan truly angry? He always had a twinkle in his eye and a joke at the ready. His jokes were more devastating than any fire-and-brimstone words could have been. Reagan's humor cut big-government liberalism and Soviet communism to the quick.

"It's hard to get an automobile in the Soviet Union," began one of my favorites. "It takes an average of ten years to get a car . . . so this man [ordered one] and the dealer said, 'Okay, in ten years, come get your car.'

" 'Morning or afternoon?' the man replied.

" 'Well, what difference does it make?' said the dealer, wondering why the time of day mattered so far into the future.

" 'The plumber is coming in the morning!' "

Reagan helped change the world by pairing his spine of steel with a smile.

We need to be happy warriors as well. Our objective is not winning arguments. It is winning converts. Thin skin and a hair trigger make us look like an angry political minority. If we want to impress the *amygdalae* and *posterior cingulate cortexes* of the American people (stay tuned to meet a neuroscientist who will explain what that means) we need to learn to debate in the spirit of charity.

So the next time you accidentally lead with the economic case against the minimum wage and someone accuses you of shilling for billionaires or hating the poor, smile and say, "Nice hit!" before you make a better argument.

But here's the catch (pun intended)—you have to actually *mean it*. Good humor has to be authentic or people see through it in an instant. Andrew Luck isn't faking it. Neither can you. To be a happy warrior you must work to be a genuinely happy person.

## 4. STEAL ALL THE BEST ARGUMENTS.

A few years back, I was delivering a speech at a big Tea Party rally. The title of my speech was "Conservative Social Justice." I laid out a host of ways in which conservatives could champion the poor, and made my moral case for why we are called to do so. Afterward, an unhappy activist approached me and began a lecture. "You can't talk about social justice," she insisted.

"Why not?"

"Because even using that language concedes the argument to the left!"

We hear variants of this all the time. If you are a conservative, there are certain code words you're supposed to use and others from which you must keep your distance. Deploy particular language and themes that make you easy to figure out. And whatever you do, stay a mile away from the signals of the other side.

This common trope is brutally bad advice. The side that wins is the side that scrambles the categories.

Americans—by significant margins—believe that "empathy" and "compassion" are traits owned by Democrats. When all the average voter knows about a candidate is that he is a Democrat, the voter instinctively assumes the guy's heart is in the right place. The left gets those two traits for free, we might say, before the campaign even begins.

Conservatives own several traits of their own. Most voters, across the ideological spectrum, instinctively associate "traditional morals" (on the social issues) and "strong leadership" with the political right. Tell a citizen nothing except a candidate's GOP affiliation, and she will assume that the candidate takes charge and believes in leading an upright life.

This is the terrain each side holds when every campaign begins. Knowing this, should conservatives double down on traditional morality and strong leadership? Reinvest in our comparative advantage? Or should we trespass on our opponent's traits, and try to launch a rhetorical sneak attack on the other team's home territory?

This question could occupy endless theoretical debate. But fortunately, we have data on the issue, and they are unambiguous. The correct strategy is to appropriate: Make the arguments for empathy and compassion.

Anyone familiar with the world of business is probably raising an eyebrow. In the private sector, success almost always comes from redoubling on natural strengths. If you own a cardboard box factory, you want to focus on making the world's best cardboard boxes. It's usually a mistake to try to dive into some new and entirely unrelated line of work.

Politicians think they should follow the same rule. Most Republicans conclude their path to victory is to be redder than red— emphasize strength and traditional social issues and forget about the soft stuff. For a long time, conventional conservative opinion has declared it a waste of time to try to persuade Americans that we have compassion for struggling people. *We have limited resources. Those people will never vote for us anyway. And the other side already owns that image. Why bother trying to trespass?*

That's a great argument, except for two tiny points: Trait-trespassing is the right thing to do and it's the only way to win nationwide.

First, it is a simple truism that patriots and leaders fight for everyone who needs them, not the subset who support them. Talk to any of our veterans who fought in Iraq or Afghanistan. They were there to defend our entire nation, to keep every single American safe—even the people who don't like or support the military. Each of us has to be a warrior in the same way. A servant leader is called to fight for every single American regardless of how they may vote.

And second, in a happy twist of fate, doing the right thing has a political payoff. Most Americans don't want to choose between compassion and morality, or between leadership and empathy. We want leaders who have all these traits.

George Washington University political scientist Danny Hayes has done groundbreaking work in this subject.[11] His research shows that Americans love a leader who throws out the usual script and competes on nontraditional moral ground. Hayes combs through decades of data. Here's what he finds: If voters rate two candidates as equally strong leaders—meaning the Democrat has erased his initial deficit on this trait—the electorate breaks roughly 60 percent to 40 percent in favor of the Democrat. Conversely, if a Republican manages to overcome the empathy gap—if voters see both the contenders as equally empathetic—he or she wins with about 65 percent.

These are huge margins, and they offer a crystal-clear takeaway: Voters reward candidates who go after unconventional traits.

There are a handful of politicians who keenly understand this. Two of them happen to share a last name. In 1992, when Bill Clinton was first running for president, members of the Los Angeles police beat a motorist named Rodney King. Riots broke out across the city. In the aftermath, a hip-hop artist named Sister Souljah gave a now-infamous interview. "If black people kill black people every day," she proposed, "why not have a week and kill white people? [If] you're a gang member and you would normally be killing somebody, why not kill a white person?"[12] Charming, I know.

Not long after Sister Souljah made those comments, Clinton was invited to speak at a conference Jesse Jackson had convened. Sister Souljah was also a speaker.[13] Clinton surprised the room when he used his platform to take Sister Souljah to task. "If you took the words 'white' and 'black,' " he lambasted, "and you reversed them, you might think [Ku Klux Klan leader] David Duke was giving that speech."[14]

This episode became known as Clinton's "Sister Souljah moment." His remarks set off a firestorm on the left, but they were a politically brilliant move. Clinton had put on a clinic in trait-trespassing. As a Democrat, he was already assumed by voters to be empathetic and compassionate. With these comments, he was staking a claim to moral leadership as well.

What about a more recent example? As Hillary Clinton was touring the country in 2014 to promote her new book, she seized a "Sister Souljah moment" of her own. She sharply criticized Barack Obama for the rise of the Islamic State. Obama's "failure" to arm and train pro-Western rebels, the former secretary of state argued, had "left a big vacuum which the jihadists have now filled." [15] Clinton even took a direct shot at the slogan the Obama administration had recently coined to describe its foreign policy doctrine: "don't do stupid [stuff]." Clinton retorted that "great nations need organizing principles, and 'don't do stupid stuff' is *not* an organizing principle."

Why did Clinton carve out such a hawkish position? Maybe she really believes it—but in any event, it was brilliant politics. As a Democrat, Clinton knows she already gets credit for the typical Democratic traits of empathy and compassion. By criticizing President Obama's national security record, she was making a play for a classic Republican characteristic—strong leadership.

The Clintons know what they are doing. When Democrats shake up the conventional categories and convey that they're serious about morality and strong on national security, they do well. They get at least as many votes from their own base, way more votes from independents, and even some votes from conservatives. The reverse will bear similar fruit. If Republicans work hard to win on empathy and compassion, they will get more votes across the political spectrum and especially from independents.

Every Republican leader needs to hammer this home. "The reason I am a conservative is because I care about poverty. I'm fighting to help the poor. And I'm going to do it whether they vote for me or not."

If we started saying that and saying it often enough—and meaning it—the data suggest massive changes. A 10 percentage point swing of independent voters to the conservative candidate is within reach.

Leaving those points on the table is political negligence of the highest order. In a tight presidential election, that margin could easily make all the difference. This is not something that can win. I believe this is the *only* thing that will win. And, most important of all, it is the right thing to do. Expand your moral imagination. Trespass on your opponent's traits.

## 5. GO WHERE YOU'RE NOT WELCOME.

Humans have a natural tendency to go where we already feel comfortable. If you are an evangelical Christian, it is most fun to hang out with other evangelicals who appreciate and share your values. I get that.

Conservatives have this tendency in spades. We tend to be very insular, talking to each other about our goals and complaining to each other about all the bad things the left is up to. At most conservative events, you will not see much exposure to centrist or liberal points of view, to say the least. And it's rarely in a leader's self-interest to expose him- or herself to gratuitous shots from the other side.

Unfortunately, people who need converting are not converted when we don't leave the house.

Our goal for the conservative movement is not to remain a motivated minority. We want to become a transformational moral majority. To do that, we need to become a more magnetic movement, attracting people who don't yet see things our way and enlisting them into our cause.

Doing that requires rethinking how we engage with three different audiences:

*True believers*—those who are already with us;
*Persuadables*—those who are not yet with us; and
*Hostiles*—those who will never be with us.

We need a clear strategy for each group. And yes, we have to spend time with all three.

First, consider the standard Republican strategy for talking to true believers. Our leaders fire people up! They get us mad! At conservative gatherings, candidates take the stage and start lobbing rhetorical raw steaks into the audience. The press reports which anti-Obama lines got the biggest applause and who got the longest standing ovations.

There's nothing wrong with firing people up. People who are fired up knock on doors, make phone calls, and turn out to vote. But there are right and wrong ways to fire people up. When we fuel the fire with negative, oppositional, and minoritarian rhetoric, we may still motivate some true believers, but we fail to make them into effective missionaries. We turn off everyone else who is listening.

Many of you, like me, may be religious converts. If that's you, I would bet almost anything that you weren't attracted to loud, apocalyptic declarations from your new faith's most fiery adherents. More likely, you encountered other true believers who carried themselves with humility, courage, and clarity of purpose. You thought to yourself, *I want what they have. I want to learn more.* This kind of magnetic attraction is how hearts are won.

How can the conservative movement acquire this magnetism? Read St. Paul's letters to the early Christians. He didn't tell them to get fired up and go attack the pagans. But he didn't instruct them to wall themselves off, either. Instead, he simply asked them to take part in their communities and be the best Christians they could possibly be. Don't argue with one another or harangue your neighbors, he wrote. Share with everyone. Love one another. Live a life worthy of the calling you have received. Living in this way is how people "put on the full armor of God."

Paul knew that by showing their true hearts to everyone, the fledgling Christians would magnetize themselves and draw in outsiders organically. Needless to say, we could stand to learn this lesson as conservatives.

The first step to put Paul's advice into practice is firing up the true believers in the right way. Forget negativity. Speak to our friends and allies in a way that encourages them, improves them, and makes them want to share their own principles of happiness and freedom with others.

A more magnetic right will also be better positioned to reach the second segment of our national audience—the "persuadables." These are Americans who are currently neither with us nor against us. They don't wake up every morning convinced that conservatives are evil. They are persuadable unless and until we drive them away.

Most persuadable people are not deeply ideological. They are looking for bold solutions and are willing to give either party a chance. Many of them voted for Barack Obama but have precious little confidence left in his leadership. They tend to be political independents who pay relatively close attention to current affairs. They give both sides a hearing. And there are millions and millions of them out there.

To approach them, we need to learn from the unconventional entrepreneurs of Silicon Valley. When a technology company like Apple unveils a new product, it is not responding to existing demand from the marketplace. It is creating brand-new demand to match brand-new supply. Before the iPhone existed, nobody had a clue they needed an iPhone. Now people wait in line overnight just to grab the latest version a few weeks ahead of everyone else in their social circle. Apple manufactured this demand by targeting early adopters. They identified and spoke directly to people who want to try something new. They consciously chose a base of customers who view themselves as independent freethinkers and want to project that image to the rest of the world.

If this sounds familiar, it's because I am describing my old self. It spurred my conversion to conservatism. I didn't enter my adulthood with any political opinions to speak of, just a kind of reflexive progressive outlook. All I had was a gut instinct that my preconceptions weren't cutting it, that I had to question everything and build a new understanding from scratch. I spent a long time as a persuadable. But unfortunately—or fortunately, I suppose, for their sanity—only a tiny percentage of persuadable Americans are crazy enough to spend a decade in school to figure out public policy for themselves.

We need a strategy to reach the rest. And to continue our extended metaphor, let's try on the very same message that technologists use to target their own persuadables: "Think different." Think for yourself.

We need to challenge these persuadables to ask questions. (If you consider yourself a persuadable, I challenge you to ask yourself these questions right now.) *Is the country headed in the right direction? Have poor people grown in prosperity since the Great Recession ended? Is it easier now than in 2008 for the majority without a college degree to find a job?* Almost everyone who looks objectively at the facts will conclude intuitively that the answers are "no." Those at the top have done just fine for the past six years, but those at the bottom are worse off. What we're doing is not working. Curious, ambitious people should not settle for this. They know we need to try new things.

We aren't asking persuadable people to become registered Republicans. We're not asking for some grand epiphany and a bulk order of this book. We're simply daring them to think different, to consider a few fresh ideas that may fall outside their zone of familiarity. In short, we have to engage these Americans like those frighteningly extroverted supermarket employees who offer bacon-wrapped samples on toothpicks to passersby. We have to fearlessly approach new people and be clear. "Just try it. That's all I'm asking you to do."

There is one more characteristic of persuadables that's especially interesting. Remember, these people pay close attention, and that doesn't only apply when you speak directly to them. They always have half an ear open. And they keenly observe how you interact with a third group of people—those who are hostile.

Hostile people *do* wake up thinking conservatives are evil or stupid. They have their minds made up. As a result, most conservatives think there's no point in engaging them. We tend to either avoid them or attack them, depending on our mood.

That is a mistake. Trying to throw bombs at hostiles and attempting to ignore them are both losing strategies. A better idea is to actually walk among them and understand them. We need to remember that even our ideological foes are human beings well worth engaging. Our goal isn't even to convert them en masse, although that would certainly be nice. We may convince a few at the margins. But more broadly, how we take a rhetorical punch will demonstrate to persuadables what kind of people we are, and indeed, remind *us* of who we are.

Of course, people who strongly disagree with us are rarely thrilled when they think we're infiltrating their territory. They often respond with vitriol and anger. That turns out to be their loss, though, because persuadable citizens are watching. Conversely, when we engage the other side with grace and answer their anger with love, the persuadables see us do it. Think of all the attention Americans pay to videos of politicians contending with hostile interviewers and hecklers. They either come across

as petty and thin-skinned or as reasonable and courageous. Inter-
acting gracefully with our political "enemies"—that is, not treat-
ing them like enemies—is key to becoming a true majority.

Besides, our own arguments will be better for it. One of the
problems with talking only to people who agree with you is that
you end up being wrong a lot. If any conservative doubts this, just
listen to how some MSNBC pundits talk about conservatives. The
problem is not that they have progressive views. The problem is
that they are *wrong* about conservatives all the time—because
they never actually spend any time with conservatives. As a result,
they mischaracterize our policies, misrepresent our priorities, and
attribute motives to us that don't actually exist.

Every conservative feels frustrated by this. And yet, when we
never interact with the other side, we often end up unintention-
ally mirroring this bad behavior. At one rally in 2012, I distinctly
remember somebody saying, "I just have *no clue* how anybody
could vote for this president again!" I am certainly no fan of the
administration, but we should not be totally mystified that anyone
might possibly disagree with us in good faith. Some on the right
are convinced that progressive policies are actually intended to
hold people back, so that poor people will become reliant on social
assistance and stay Democratic voters forever. But the truth is that
most liberals do want to help the poor—they just have the wrong
ideas about how to do it. We should not be like the ideologues on
television and ascribe evil motives to our opponents. Most of the
time, this is flat-out wrong, and it makes us seem just as out of
touch as they are. These are errors, and our persuadable audience
is watching.

We need to better understand what motivates the other side.
If we don't, we are going to be wrong about them the same way
we're sure they are wrong about us. We are called to find common
ground where it genuinely exists, improve our own arguments,

and win over persuadable Americans by answering hostility with magnanimity, understanding, good humor, and love.

## 6. SAY IT IN THIRTY SECONDS.

Gut instincts, love at first sight—all my life, I'd thought that snap judgments about others were silly and impulsive. I considered them a mark of shallow thinking. But then one day, I made just that sort of snap judgment, and it changed my life for good.

In the summer of 1988, at the age of twenty-four, I was traveling around the Burgundy region of France. This wasn't some "find-yourself" backpacking trip; I was working. I was touring and recording at the time with a brass quintet. For a couple of weeks that July, we were playing concerts in and around the city of Dijon.

The first night I arrived, I took the stage and squinted out at a small audience. (In retrospect, it seems like all the audiences were small, which may be why I was barely making rent.) My gaze was drawn to the front row, and there I spotted a girl with black hair and dark eyes. She smiled at me. So, being a pretty typical twenty-four-year-old male, I made a mental note to talk to her when the concert finished.

That turned out to be no easy task. As soon as the performance ended, I made a beeline in her direction. I took a deep breath, marched up, and introduced myself. Turns out she spoke no English. She was Spanish, studying in France that summer. I spoke no Spanish. Our "conversation" was a ridiculous combination of hand gestures and monosyllabic words with international meaning.

Here's the odd thing I remember about that night. When I first began speaking with her, a thought appeared in my mind seemingly from out of nowhere:

"I would like to marry this girl."

Now, you have to understand that getting married was pretty far from my mind at that point. It was weirder still, because we were having next to no meaningful verbal interaction. She could have told me, "I am a serial killer and you look like a nice victim," and I would have had no idea.

But "I want to marry her" is what popped into my head after just a few seconds. And it stayed there. I actually told my parents a few weeks later that I had met the girl I was going to marry, without even having the language skills to tell the girl herself.

How did that one turn out? Long story short: Today we have been married for almost twenty-four years, and have three kids.

A couple of years into our marriage, in the Spanglish that had grown into the private language we still use today, I told her of my snap judgment at our first meeting and asked what *she* was thinking at that moment. "I thought you were trying too hard," she told me. So much for mutual spontaneous attraction.

Believe it or not, that story has something to do with the future of the conservative movement. What I got that night in France, in addition to a lifelong partner, was a crash course in brain science. I learned that I could form a shockingly complete opinion of others based on the first impression. And what was true for me the moment I met my future wife is true for people who are first hearing the new right's pitch for America. We have just a few seconds to make our case.


Daniela Schiller is not your average neuroscientist. By day, she is director of the Schiller Laboratory of Affective Neuroscience at the Mount Sinai School of Medicine in New York City. By night, she is the drummer for the Amygdaloids, a rock band made up of neuroscientists. They got started by covering songs about mental disorders (think of the Rolling Stones' "19th Nervous Breakdown") and eventually began producing original material.

When she is not performing in front of thousands of people, Schiller is designing groundbreaking studies that investigate the inner workings of the human mind. In 2009, she led a fascinating brain study with some colleagues at New York University.

Volunteers underwent a brain scan while they were shown pictures of male faces. Each face was followed by six sentences that described a good or bad action supposedly performed by that person. For example, a picture of a young man might be accompanied by a description of a favor he did for a friend, such as not smoking in front of him while he was trying to quit (good), or an insult he hurled out the window of his car (bad). They showed the same faces to each subject but varied the positive or negative information paired with each. This ensured they were examining subjects' brain reactions to the little stories and not simply to looks.

Schiller and her fellow researchers were interested in how the brains of the participants apprehended this information to make a judgment. They found that two brain regions were activated and led to judgments within seconds: the *amygdala* (the region for which her band is named, which assigns emotional values) and the *posterior cingulate cortex* (which is involved in the coding of values and emotional memory). Both of these brain regions are found deep in the center of the brain, and are evolutionarily ancient. That means that long before people had today's reasoning capacity, they possessed these structures to help them assess others.

Half a million years ago—before the advent of laws, police, well-ordered societies, or even well-developed languages—it was no easy task to distinguish friends from foes. Was a stranger a relative or a competitor? Should I flee from an unexpected visitor, fight him, or welcome him into my cave? Get it wrong and the consequences could be deadly. Those with the best judgment were most likely to pass on their genes.

Fast-forward to the present. Today our modern, reasoning brains still have this ancient mechanism. It whispers to our subconscious whether somebody we meet in a Dijon concert hall (or see on television) is a friend or a foe. "When you are exposed to information or someone speaks to you, there is already activation of brain systems that are involved in evaluation and emotional reaction," Schiller says. "In social situations, there are so many cues that we rely heavily on these very quick automatic processes."

"We're not even aware that we make these decisions," she explains. But "people make very fast judgments and usually they are very persistent." [16]

How fast? The study states, "People make relatively accurate and persistent evaluations on the basis of rapid observations of even less than half a minute." [17]

Once you make a bad impression, it's very difficult to recover. "If you associate a person with something negative, even by accident—maybe because you didn't like the person's face or their particular expression in that moment—you immediately create an association with that person, and then it's pretty hard to change these associations," Schiller says. It can be done, of course: "The more developed parts of the cortex can inhibit the very basic activation of the more fundamental automatic reaction." But doing so "would take a lot more effort" and is "a taxing process."

In other words, science verifies the old cliché that "there's no second chance to make a good first impression."

This is yet another reason why explaining economics to everybody does not work. It simply takes too long. We think we have thirty minutes to lead people to a logical conclusion. In reality, we have less than thirty seconds.

This explains my snap judgment about my future wife. It was

an ancient part of my brain reading out a message—"friendly." On her end, the same factors explain why she didn't run away in fear. Thank you, amygdala!

This is information you can use. Want to nail your next job interview? Focus on the first thirty seconds. Now we know why eye contact matters right off the bat, as does an authentic smile. It's not that your future boss is shallow. It's that his posterior cingulate cortex and amygdala are summing you up while his conscious brain is still thinking about lunch. For the next hour you might talk about your last job, the college you went to, or what you like to do in your spare time. It might be a great conversation. But still, he leaves the interview with the sensation that something about you just isn't quite right. His amygdala subconsciously sabotaged you for your wimpy handshake.

Want to radically improve your public speaking? You could go to a class where they will tell you to speak slowly, summarize your points at the end, and a thousand other things. But the real secret is getting the opening of the speech right. A great speech treats the first opening seconds like the scarce and valuable commodity that they are.

Great orators in history understood this. Consider the very first words of Abraham Lincoln's Gettysburg Address:

*Four score and seven years ago our fathers brought forth on this continent a new nation, conceived in liberty, and dedicated to the proposition that all men are created equal.*

Or take the opening of Martin Luther King Jr.'s "I Have a Dream" speech:

*I am happy to join with you today in what will go down in history as the greatest demonstration for freedom in the history of our nation.*

Neither Lincoln nor King was a neuroscientist. Yet they both understood the first priority in making a good impression on others: Don't blow your opening lines.

Note, by the way, *how* Lincoln and King used their opening lines. As our previous habits have made clear, a compelling pitch needs to be explicitly moral and focus on fighting for people. Lincoln spoke in his opening seconds about liberty and equality for all men. King spoke straight to the need for universal freedom. That is why these men were iconic communicators. That is why these speeches changed the nation. Still today, these speeches affect the deep brains of all those who listen to them. And all that is possible because each man's first thirty seconds keep us eagerly listening.

Today's leaders must remember this. Each of us has ancient regions in our brain that make us decide if that politician on TV is a friend or foe. If our brain says he or she's a friend, we're going to keep listening. If it says he or she's a foe, we're going to tune out. We're going to make our decision very quickly, and we're not even going to know why.

Some object that you can't make a compelling political case in that short a time. Yes, you can. In the 1990s, the Democratic strategist Paul Begala was trying to get his candidate Harris Wofford to do it. Wofford, who was running for the U.S. Senate in Pennsylvania on a platform to reform health care, told his advisor, "My health-care plan is too complicated to explain in a sound bite." So Begala pulled out a Bible, turned to John 3:16, and asked Wofford to read it aloud. Wofford took the Bible and read:

> *For God so loved the world that He gave His only begotten Son, that whoever believes in him shall not perish but have eternal life.*

The verse took just eight seconds to recite. Triumphantly, Begala told him, "If God can explain Christianity in eight seconds, you can explain your health-care plan."

If God can explain Christianity in eight seconds, thirty seconds should be more than enough for us to explain what animates the conservative heart.

## 7. BREAK YOUR BAD HABITS.

For a long time, the list of tactics I'd share with congressmen, senators, and other conservative communicators used to have only six items. But then I noticed a pattern. Policymakers with whom I had worked were coming back to report in, and they often said some version of this: "I wrote down those things you said. I went out ready to use them. But then, when I got into a debate, I panicked and went back to all my old arguments and attacks. I guess I'm just no good at this stuff."

Can they really learn to communicate in new ways? Indeed they can, and so can we. But to change old habits, we need one last assist from the world of neuroscience, and a part of the brain called the *basal ganglia*. It's a nub of neurological tissue that until recently scientists did not understand very well. But now researchers believe it may play a huge role in how we form habits.

In his fascinating book *The Power of Habit*, science reporter Charles Duhigg of the *New York Times* shows that good habits—from brushing our teeth to concentrating on our work—are emphatically within our reach. Bad habits like smoking and cussing are all breakable. It's not even that hard.

Duhigg details dozens of brain studies. They show that habits are behaviors that bypass our conscious thought and are processed by the basal ganglia. To illustrate, he points to work back in the 1990s, when researchers at the Massachusetts Institute of Technology examined rats in a maze who were looking for chocolate. When the animals are first put into the maze, their little brains go crazy. The rats sniff the air, make wrong turns, go down blind alleys, and have to start over—the learning parts of their brains are in overdrive. But as they learn the routine, their brains calm down and the basal ganglia take over. The rats train themselves to race straight for the chocolate without any conscious activity. More reward, less work, no conscious thought. That's a habit.

The basal ganglia work the same way in humans. There are documented cases of brain injury in which patients became unable to remember simple tasks and facts, such as being able to name where they live. Yet in practice, they are perfectly capable of finding their way home from any point in the neighborhood. That's because their habit center is in charge, not their memory or executive function.

Conversely, when the basal ganglia are damaged, the results are catastrophic. Cases of this make people's lives impossible. Even if unimpaired in all other ways, they can't figure out how to turn a doorknob or tie their shoes. They can't figure out facial expressions or discern cues from others.

So the key to quitting bad habits and building good habits is to reprogram the amazing basal ganglia. Want to quit smoking? It's not easy, but conceptually it is pretty simple. Use your executive brain to interrupt your routine and substitute a good habit for the bad one. When you have a desire to light up, you should still get up and head outside—but once you're there, just walk around. Do this a few thousand times and you will be an ex-smoker with new programming deep in your brain's habit center. You won't even have to think about it anymore. I know because I have personally lived this example. At first I thought it was impossible. Today, I almost never think about smoking.

So it will be with you, too, as you adopt a new way of thinking and talking about the issues you care about. When you are about to argue that the main benefit of free enterprise is that it creates economic growth, you just pulled out a rhetorical cigarette. Bad habit. Catch yourself and substitute your new argument in its place—one that starts with a moral statement, fights for people, and maybe trespasses on the other side's traits. Sooner than you think, you will be the person who automatically appeals to compassion and fairness in the first thirty seconds. And you will start winning the argument.

## THE CONSERVATIVE HEART

We've covered a lot of dimensions of the conservative heart in this book: the pursuit of happiness, the solution to poverty, the blessings of work, the fight for social justice, the need for a social movement. And in this chapter, the keys to effective communication.

We are almost done, but I need to make one final point. This book—especially this chapter—can easily be mistaken for a manual of rhetorical tricks to fool and dazzle: "Get anyone to do anything!" But that is manifestly *not* what I've argued. The point is not to fool people into voting against their interests, but to make us better at expressing the content of our own characters so we become better servants for people in need.

The world needs us to stop losing. There are too many people in America who are being left behind. There are too many people overseas who don't enjoy the benefits of democratic capitalism and free enterprise. There are too many people everywhere who have been denied the happiness that comes with earned success. Those people need us. If we want the chance to help them, we've got to improve the way we make our case to the American people.

We have to share what is written on the conservative heart.

# ACKNOWLEDGMENTS

Many people helped make this book a reality, but none more than my AEI colleagues Marc Thiessen and Andrew Quinn. Many sections of this book started as conversations with Marc, who expanded, improved, and converted them into written prose. And if readers find the book entertaining, I have Andy's research and editing artistry to thank.

I am indebted to Adam Bellow, my editor at Broadside Books, and to Lisa Adams, my literary agent at the Garamond Agency. Several of the key ideas in this book—especially the chapter on happiness—were developed on the pages of the *New York Times*, and I am grateful to my editor Trish Hall. Thanks also to John Podhoretz, editor of *Commentary* magazine, where the chapter on social justice began its life.

My AEI colleagues—my fellow warriors for freedom and opportunity—are a constant source of inspiration. Leading AEI is the greatest honor of my professional life. Special thanks for their help on this project go to my colleagues Jason Bertsch, John Cusey, Sadanand Dhume, Robert Doar, Nick Eberstadt, Cecilia Gallogly, David Gerson, Kevin Hassett, Justin Lang, Rachel Manfredi, Charles Murray, Mark Perry, and Michael Strain.

I am grateful for the trust and support of my friend and AEI's Chairman, Tully Friedman, AEI's outstanding board of trustees, and its steadfast and generous donors. For support on this project, all of us at AEI would like to thank the Kern Family Foundation, the Anschutz Foundation, the Marcus Foundation, the Doug and Maria DeVos Foundation, the Richard and Helen DeVos Foundation, the Dick and Betsy DeVos Foundation, the Morgridge Family Foundation, the Charles Koch Foundation, the Triad Foundation, George Roberts, Seth Klarman, Kelli and Allen Questrom, Jack and Pina Templeton, and Art and Carlyse Ciocca.

I am particularly indebted to my intellectual partner and wife, Ester Munt-Brooks. As an American by choice instead of by birth, Ester constantly reminds me why our American society and system are a gift not to be taken for granted. And I owe thanks to our three children, Joaquim, Carlos, and Marina, who have gotten used to that haunted look Dad gets when he is working on a book.

This book is dedicated in memory of James Q. Wilson, a great patriot, scholar, and mentor. Jim was a motivational and generous force at each juncture of my career, and a living example of the Conservative Heart.

All royalties from the sale of this book go to support the work of the American Enterprise Institute.

# NOTES

## Introduction

1     Maxim Pinkovskiy and Xavier Sala-i-Martin, "Parametric Estimations of the World Distribution of Income," NBER Working Paper No. 15433 (October 2009), doi:10.3386/w15433.

2     "Global Poverty Is on the Decline, but Almost No One Believes It," Barna Group, accessed March 27, 2015, https://www.barna.org/barna-update/culture /668-global-poverty-is-on-the-decline-but-almost-no-one-believes-it.

3     "Satisfaction with the United States," Gallup, accessed January 8, 2015, http://www.gallup.com/poll/1669/general-mood-country.aspx.

4     "The AP-GfK Poll," GfK Public Affairs, accessed December 8, 2014, http:// ap-gfkpoll.com/main/wp-content/uploads/2013/10/AP-GfK-October-2013 -Poll-Topline-Final_VIEWS.pdf.

5     This is a central theme of Jonathan Haidt, *The Righteous Mind: Why Good People Are Divided by Politics and Religion* (New York: Pantheon Books, 2012). See also Jesse Graham, Jonathan Haidt, and Brian A. Nosek, "Liberals and Conservatives Rely on Different Sets of Moral Foundations," *Journal of Personality and Social Psychology* 96, doi:10.1037/a0015141.

6     Lionel Trilling, *The Liberal Imagination* (New York: Viking Press, 1950), ix.

## Chapter 1: America's Pursuit of Happiness

1     Much of the material in this section was initially developed in four of my *New York Times* essays. See Arthur C. Brooks, "Abundance Without Attachment," *New York Times*, December 14, 2014, http://www.nytimes.com/2014/12/14 /opinion/sunday/arthur-c-brooks-abundance-without-attachment.html; Arthur C. Brooks, "Love People, Not Pleasure," *New York Times*, July 18, 2014, http://www.nytimes.com/2014/07/20/opinion/sunday/arthur-c-brooks-love -people-not-pleasure.html; Arthur C. Brooks, "A Formula for Happiness," *New York Times*, December 15, 2013, http://www.nytimes.com/2013/12/15

/opinion/sunday/a-formula-for-happiness.html; Arthur C. Brooks, "Capitalism and the Dalai Lama," *New York Times*, April 18, 2014, http://www.nytimes.com/2014/04/18/opinion/capitalism-and-the-dalai-lama.html.

2 Thomas Jefferson to Henry Lee, May 8, 1825, in *The Basic Writings of Thomas Jefferson*, edited by Philip S. Foner (New York: Halcyon House, 1950), 802.

3 These figures are remarkably consistent in wave after wave of the General Social Survey (GSS). For more in-depth discussion of these GSS data, see Arthur C. Brooks, *Gross National Happiness* (New York: Basic Books, 2008).

4 Betsey Stevenson and Justin Wolfers, "The Paradox of Declining Female Happiness," NBER Working Paper No. 14969 (May 2009), doi:10.3386/w14969.

5 The author's analysis of 2012 GSS data. For particular discussion of these figures, see Andrew C. Quinn, "Sex, Politics, and Happiness in the General Social Survey," AEI Ideas blog, December 20, 2013, http://www.aei.org/publication/sex-politics-and-happiness-in-the-general-social-survey/.

6 David Lykken and Auke Tellegen, "Happiness Is a Stochastic Phenomenon," *Psychological Science* 7, no. 3 (May 1996), accessed December 7, 2014, http://www.psych.umn.edu/psylabs/happiness/happy.htm.

7 Ibid. See also Jan-Emmanuel De Neve, James H. Fowler, and Bruno S. Frey, "Genes, Economics, and Happiness," CESifo Working Paper No. 2946 (2010), accessed November 15, 2014, http://hdl.handle.net/10419/30746.

8 This is my original approximation based on the available literature. The finding that about half of happiness is heritable is a mainstream finding; see note 7 above. Lykken and Tellegen also state that the heritable portion of overall happiness (roughly half) equals about 80 percent of the stable component of happiness; the underlying math, then, leaves about 60 percent of total happiness that is not stable. This ballpark conclusion is supported by other research in the field, such as Richard E. Lucas and M. Brent Donnellan, "How Stable Is Happiness? Using the STARTS Model to Estimate the Stability of Life Satisfaction," *Journal of Research in Personality* 41, no. 5 (October 2009), doi:10.1016/j.jrp.2006.11.005. These authors estimate that roughly 37 percent of happiness likely derives from "contextual circumstances."

9 Philip Brickman, Dan Coates, and Ronnie Janoff-Bulman, "Lottery Winners and Accident Victims: Is Happiness Relative?" *Journal of Personality and Social Psychology* 36, no. 8 (1978): 917–27.

10 Author's calculations; data from the 2012 GSS.

11 Brooks, *Gross National Happiness*, 122.

12 Daniel Kahneman and Angus Deaton, "High Income Improves Evaluation of Life but Not Emotional Well-being," *PNAS* 107, no. 38 (September 21, 2010): 16489–93.

13 Author's calculations; data from the 2012 GSS.

14    Cristobal Young, "Losing a Job: The Nonpecuniary Cost of Unemployment in the United States," *Social Forces* (2012), doi:10.1093/sf/sos071.

15    Dean Baker and Kevin Hassett, "The Human Disaster of Unemployment," *New York Times*, May 12, 2012, accessed November 1, 2014, http://www.nytimes.com/2012/05/13/opinion/sunday/the-human-disaster-of-unemployment.html.

16    Richard Fletcher, *Moorish Spain*, 2nd ed. (Berkeley: University of California Press, 2006), 53–54.

17    Quote retrieved from "Happiness," Bartleby.com, accessed March 3, 2015, at http://www.bartleby.com/349/223.html.

18    Interested readers can take the quiz for themselves at https://www.authentichappiness.sas.upenn.edu/testcenter.

19    "Discrimination Is Associated with Depression Among Minority Children," *American Academy of Pediatrics*, May 3, 2010, accessed February 7, 2015, http://www.sciencedaily.com/releases/2010/05/100502080240.htm.

20    Colleen M. Heflin and John Iceland, "Poverty, Material Hardship and Depression," *Social Science Quarterly* 90, no. 5 (December 2009), doi:10.1111/j.1540-6237.2009.00645.x. Vijaya Murali and Femi Oyebode, "Poverty, Social Inequality, and Mental Health," *BJPsych Advances* 10, no. 3 (May 2004), doi:10.1192/apt.10.3.161.

21    Daniel Kahneman, Alan B. Krueger, David A. Schkade, Norbert Schwarz, and Arthur A. Stone, "A Survey Method for Characterizing Daily Life Experience: The Day Reconstruction Method," *Science* 306, no. 5702 (December 2004), doi:10.1126/science.1103572.

22    Christopher P. Niemiec, "The Path Taken: Consequences of Attaining Intrinsic and Extrinsic Aspirations in Post-College Life," *Journal of Research in Personality* 43, no. 3 (June 2009), 291–306.

23    Donna Rockwell, "Mindfulness in Everyday Life—So You Want to Be Famous? What You Need to Know About Celebrity," *Huffington Post*, accessed March 15, 2015, http://www.huffingtonpost.com/donna-rockwell-psyd/mindfulness-in-everyday-l_2_b_4818606.html.

24    David G. Blanchflower and Andrew J. Oswald, "Money, Sex and Happiness: An Empirical Study," *Scandinavian Journal of Economics* 106, no. 3 (September 2004), 393–415.

25    Daniel Kahneman and Angus Deaton, "High Income Improves Evaluation of Life but Not Emotional Well-being," *PNAS* 107, no. 38 (September 21, 2010): 16489–93.

26    Researchers have vividly measured the principle of adaptation using a method called the Leyden Approach: They ask people what income levels they would consider to be "very bad," "bad," "insufficient," "sufficient," "good," and "very good." The studies find that, no matter what your income, the level

halfway between insufficient and sufficient (your "required income") is about 40 percent higher than what you make right now. If you earn $50,000 per year, your required income is $70,000. But if you get a raise to $70,000, your required income will very quickly jump to about $98,000. See Bernard M. S. Van Praag and Paul Frijters, "The Measurement of Welfare and Well-Being," in *Well-Being: The Foundations of Hedonic Psychology*, edited by Daniel Kahneman, Ed Diener, and Norbert Schwarz (New York: Russell Sage, 1999), 413–33.

27   Leaf Van Boven, and Thomas Gilovich, "To Do or to Have? That Is the Question," *Journal of Personality and Social Psychology* 85, no. 6 (2003): 1193–1202.

28   Thich Nhat Hanh, *The Miracle of Mindfulness* (London: Rider Books, 2008), 3.

29   Edward L. Deci and Richard M. Ryan, *Intrinsic Motivation and Self-Determination in Human Behavior* (New York: Plenum Press, 1985).

30   Fr. Robert Barron, "You're Holier Than You Know," *U.S. Catholic*, July 2008, accessed January 13, 2015, http://www.uscatholic.org/church/2008/07 /youre-holier-you-know.

### Chapter 2: Why America Hasn't Won the War on Poverty

1   Charles Murray, "The New American Divide," *Wall Street Journal*, January 21, 2012, accessed February 22, 2014, http://www.wsj.com/articles/SB10001 424052970204301404577170733817181646.

2   Charles Murray, *Coming Apart: The State of White America, 1960–2010* (New York: Crown Forum, 2012).

3   Author's original calculations; data from the 2010 General Social Survey.

4   Leon Dash, "Rosa Lee's Story: About the Series," *Washington Post* (1994), accessed November 8, 2015, http://www.washingtonpost.com/wp-srv/local /longterm/library/rosalee/backgrnd.htm.

5   My too-brief summary of Rosa Lee Cunningham's life draws from all eight stories in Leon Dash's masterful multipart series. For a complete table of contents and links to all eight pieces, readers can visit the *Washington Post*'s website. As of March 2015, the series is available at http://www.washingtonpost .com/wp-srv/local/longterm/library/rosalee/backgrnd.htm.

6   Leon Dash, "A Life Comes Full Circle, and Rosa Lee Faces Loss (Part Eight)," *Washington Post*, September 25, 1994, accessed November 8, 2014, http://www.washingtonpost.com/wp-srv/local/longterm/library/rosalee/part 8.htm.

7   Leon Dash, "Daughter Travels the Same Troubled Path (Part Six)," *Washington Post*, September 23, 1994, accessed November 8, 2014, http://www.wash ingtonpost.com/wp-srv/local/longterm/library/rosalee/part6.htm.

8    Leon Dash, "A Difficult Journey (Part One)," *Washington Post*, September 18, 1994, accessed November 8, 2014, http://www.washingtonpost.com/wp-srv /local/longterm/library/rosalee/part1.htm.

9    "The Readers React," *Washington Post*, October 2, 1994, accessed November 8, 2014, http://www.washingtonpost.com/wp-srv/local/longterm/library /rosalee/readers.htm.

10    Lyndon B. Johnson, Annual Message to the Congress on the State of the Union, January 8, 1964, accessed March 2, 2015, http://www.presidency.ucsb .edu/ws/?pid=26787.

11    Lyndon B. Johnson, "The Great Society" (remarks at the University of Michigan), May 22, 1964, accessed March 2, 2015, http://www.pbs.org/wgbh /americanexperience/features/primary-resources/lbj-michigan/.

12    "War on Poverty: Portraits from an Appalachian Battlefield, 1964," *Life*, accessed March 2, 2014, at http://life.time.com/history/war-on-poverty-appa lachia-portraits-1964/.

13    Mollie Orshansky, "The Poor in City and Suburb, 1964," *Social Security Bulletin* (December 1966): 22–37, http://www.ssa.gov/policy/docs/ssb/v29n12 /v29n12p22.pdf.

14    Ibid.

15    Nicholas Eberstadt, "The Great Society at Fifty," *Weekly Standard*, May 19, 2014, accessed February 12, 2015, http://www.weeklystandard.com /articles/great-society-fifty_791175.html?page=3.

16    Robert Rector and Rachel Sheffield, "The War on Poverty After 50 Years," Heritage Foundation, September 15, 2014, accessed February 12, 2015, http:// www.heritage.org/research/reports/2014/09/the-war-on-poverty-after-50 -years.

17    Ibid.

18    Cameron Steagall, "The Price of Living: From 1964 to 2014," CBS New York, January 17, 2014, accessed February 12, 2015, http://newyork.cbslocal .com/top-lists/the-price-of-living-from-1964-to-2014/.

19    "Product Info," Best Buy, accessed February 12, 2015, http://www.best buy.com/site/insignia-39-class-38-1-2-diag—led-720p-hdtv-black/2125035.p ?id=1219068846563&skuId=2125035.

20    "Poverty in the United States: Frequently Asked Questions," National Poverty Center, accessed February 12, 2015, http://www.npc.umich.edu/pov erty/.

21    "National Income and Product Accounts Tables: 1950–1959," Bureau of Economic Analysis, accessed March 2, 2015, http://www.bea.gov/iTable/iTable Html.cfm?reqid=9&step=3&isuri=1&904=1959&903=1&906=a&905=1950&9 10=x&911=0.

22   "National Income and Product Accounts Tables: 1960–1969," Bureau of Economic Analysis, accessed March 2, 2015, http://www.bea.gov/iTable/iTable .cfm?reqid=9&step=3&isuri=1&904=1969&903=1&906=a&905=1960&910=x &911=0#reqid=9&step=3&isuri=1&904=1969&903=1&906=a&905=1960&91 0=x&911=0.

23   Sarah Kliff, "When Medicare Launched, Nobody Had Any Clue Whether It Would Work," *Washington Post*, May 17, 2013, accessed February 12, 2015, http://www.washingtonpost.com/blogs/wonkblog/wp/2013/05/17/when-medi care-launched-nobody-had-any-clue-whether-it-would-work/.

24   Carmen DeNavas-Walt and Bernadette D. Proctor, "Income and Poverty in the United States: 2013," United States Census Bureau (September 2014), http://www.census.gov/content/dam/Census/library/publications/2014/demo /p60-249.pdf.

25   Nicholas Eberstadt, "The Great Society at Fifty," *Weekly Standard*, May 19, 2014, accessed February 12, 2015, http://www.weeklystandard.com/print/arti cles/great-society-fifty_791175.html?page=2.

26   Lyndon B. Johnson, Remarks Upon Signing the Economic Opportunity Act, August 20, 1964, accessed February 12, 2015, http://www.presidency.ucsb .edu/ws/?pid=26452.

27   Bryan Altman, "Prediction Machine Picks Seahawks Over Patriots in Super Bowl XLIX," CBS Seattle, January 27, 2015, accessed February 12, 2015, http://seattle.cbslocal.com/2015/01/27/prediction-machine-picks-seahawks -over-patriots-in-super-bowl-xlix/.

28   Barbara Vobejda, "Clinton Signs Welfare Bill Amid Division," *Washington Post*, August 23, 1996, accessed February 12, 2015, http://www.washington post.com/wp-srv/politics/special/welfare/stories/wf082396.htm.

29   Bill Clinton, "How We Ended Welfare, Together," *New York Times*, August 22, 2006, accessed February 12, 2015, http://www.nytimes.com/2006 /08/22/opinion/22clinton.html.

30   John Ifcher, "The Pursuit of Happiness: How Working Mothers Feel After Welfare Reform," Leavey School of Business, Santa Clara University, accessed February 12, 2015, http://www.scu.edu/business/mindwork/archives/spring08 /ifcher.cfm.

31   John Ifcher and Homa Zarghamee, "Trends in the Happiness of Single Mothers: Evidence from the General Social Survey," Leavey School of Business, Santa Clara University (2011), accessed March 22, 2015, http://www.scu.edu/ business/economics/research/upload/TrendsinHappinessofSingleMothers.pdf.

32   Robert Rector, "Obama's End Run on Welfare Reform, Part One: Understanding Workfare," Heritage Foundation Backgrounder #2730, accessed March 28, 2015, http://www.heritage.org/research/reports/2012/09/obamas -end-run-on-welfare-reform-part-one-understanding-workfare#_ftn6, note 6.

33     Martin Feldstein, "The Global Impact of America's Housing Crisis," National Bureau of Economic Research (August 2009), accessed March 2, 2015, http://www.nber.org/feldstein/projectsyndicate082009.pdf.

34     Chris Isidore, "America's Lost Trillions," *CNN Money*, June 9, 2011, accessed February 12, 2015, http://money.cnn.com/2011/06/09/news/economy/household_wealth/.

35     "^GSPC Historic Prices," *Yahoo Finance*, accessed February 12, 2015, http://finance.yahoo.com/q/hp?s=^GSPC&a=00&b=1&c=2006&d=00&e=1&f=2010&g=d.

36     Tyler Atkinson, David Luttrell, and Harvey Rosenblum, "How Bad Was It? The Costs and Consequences of the 2007–09 Financial Crisis," *Staff Papers* 20 (2013), accessed March 2, 2015, https://dallasfed.org/assets/documents/research/staff/staff1301.pdf; Isidore, "America's Lost Trillions."

37     Kelly Greene, Liam Pleven, Laura Saunders, Dawn Wotapka, and Jason Zweig, "What We Learned from the Financial Crisis," *Wall Street Journal*, September 13, 2013, accessed February 12, 2015, http://online.wsj.com/articles/SB10001424127887323864604579069661042932546; "The Financial Crisis Response in Charts," United States Department of the Treasury (April 2012), http://www.treasury.gov/resource-center/data-chart-center/Documents/20120413_FinancialCrisisResponse.pdf.

38     Daniel Halper, "Report: U.S. Spent $3.7 Trillion on Welfare Over Last 5 Years," *Weekly Standard*, October 23, 2014, accessed February 12, 2015, http://www.weeklystandard.com/blogs/report-us-spent-37-trillion-welfare-over-last-5-years_764582.html.

39     Mark M. Gray, "Is Everyone Lining Up to Challenge Hillary Clinton Catholic?" Nineteen Sixty-Four blog, Center for Applied Research in the Apostolate, Georgetown University, accessed February 12, 2015, http://nineteensixty-four.blogspot.com/2013/06/is-everyone-lining-up-to-challenge.html. Gray tabulated his data from the American Presidency Project archives.

40     Barack Obama, "Remarks by the President on Economic Mobility," Office of the Press Secretary, December 4, 2013, accessed February 12, 2015, http://www.whitehouse.gov/the-press-office/2013/12/04/remarks-president-economic-mobility.

41     "Obama Calls Income Gap 'Wrong'—After Widening It," Investors.com, July 30, 2013, accessed February 12, 2015, http://news.investors.com/ibd-editorials/073013-665705-income-gap-grew-sharply-under-obama.htm.

42     Barack Obama, "Remarks by the President at the Associated Press Luncheon," Office of the Press Secretary, April 3, 2012, accessed February 12, 2015, https://www.whitehouse.gov/the-press-office/2012/04/03/remarks-president-associated-press-luncheon.

43   Edward N. Wolff, "The Asset Price Meltdown and the Wealth of the Middle Class," National Bureau of Economic Research (November 2012), accessed February 12, 2015, doi: 10.3386/w18559.

44   Emmanuel Saez, "Striking It Richer: The Evolution of Top Incomes in the United States (updated with 2012 preliminary estimates)," University of California, Berkeley, Department of Economics (September 3, 2013), accessed February 12, 2015, http://eml.berkeley.edu/~saez/saez-UStopincomes-2012.pdf.

45   DeNavas-Walt and Proctor, "Income and Poverty in the United States: 2013."

46   "Supplemental Nutrition Assistance Program Participation and Costs," Food and Nutrition Service, updated March 6, 2015, accessed March 2, 2015, http://www.fns.usda.gov/sites/default/files/pd/SNAPsummary.pdf.

47   Beth Laurence, "How Much in Social Security Disability Benefits Can You Get," Disability Secrets, accessed February 12, 2015, http://www.disability secrets.com/how-much-in-ssd.html.

48   "Gap in U.S. Unemployment Rates Between Rich and Poor Continues to Widen," NJ.com, September 16, 2013, accessed February 12, 2015, http://www .nj.com/business/index.ssf/2013/09/gaps_in_us_unemployment_rates.html.

49   "Economic News Release: Employment Status of the Civilian Population by Race, Sex, and Age," Bureau of Labor Statistics, updated March 6, 2015, accessed March 15, 2015, http://www.bls.gov/news.release/empsit.t02.htm.

50   Robert A. Margo, "Employment and Unemployment in the 1930s," *Journal of Economic Perspectives* 7, no. 2 (1993): 41–59, https://fraser.stlouisfed.org /docs/meltzer/maremp93.pdf.

51   Emily Swanson, "Poll: Republican Party Wants to Help the Rich," *Huffington Post*, September 25, 2013, accessed February 12, 2015, http://www.huff ingtonpost.com/2013/09/25/republican-party-rich_n_3984789.html.

52   "As Midterms Near, GOP Leads on Key Issues, Democrats Have a More Positive Image," Pew Research Center (October 23, 2014), accessed February 12, 2015, http://www.people-press.org/2014/10/23/as-midterms-near-gop-leads-on -key-issues-democrats-have-a-more-positive-image/.

### Chapter 3: Pushing the Bucket

1   "Remarks of 2011 Ready, Willing & Able Graduate Dallas Davis," You-Tube video, April 5, 2011, accessed March 1, 2015, https://www.youtube.com /watch?v=XMXSIx2L1AA.

2   "Mama Doe Candlelight Vigil," Doe Fund, accessed March 10, 2015, http://www.doe.org/events_past_detail.cfm?eventID=146.

3   Associated Press, "Homeless Woman Found Dead in Grand Central Terminal," December 26, 1985, accessed March 10, 2015, http://www.doe.org /news_detail.cfm?pressID=60&news_type=archives.

4    Sandra Yin, "Doe Fund Plays Role in Changing Lives," March 23, 2000, accessed March 10, 2015, http://www.doe.org/news_detail.cfm?pressID=12& news_type=archives.

5    "Deputy Attorney General James M. Cole Speaks at the Southeastern Regional Reentry Conference," October 16, 2012, http://www.justice.gov/opa /speech/deputy-attorney-general-james-m-cole-speaks-southeastern-regional -reentry-conference.

6    Joan Petersilia, "When Prisoners Return to the Community: Political, Economic, and Social Consequences," *Papers from the Executive Sessions on Sentencing and Corrections* 9 (November 2000), U.S. Department of Justice, https://www.ncjrs.gov/pdffiles1/nij/184253.pdf.

7    Catherine Sirois and Bruce Western, "An Evaluation of Ready, Willing, and Able," Action Research Report, Harvard University (2010).

8    Andy Kiersz, "Labor Force Participation Falls to Its Lowest Rate Since 1978," *Business Insider,* October 3, 2014, accessed March 18, 2015, http://www .businessinsider.com/labor-force-participation-rate-september-2014-2014-10.

9    Yian Q. Mui, "More Americans Are Stuck in Part-time Work," *Washington Post,* July 3, 2014, accessed March 3, 2015, http://www.washingtonpost .com/business/economy/more-americans-are-stuck-in-part-time-work/2014 /07/02/2eefaa72-f7e7-11e3-a3a5-42be35962a52_story.html.

10    Author's original calculations; data from the 2001 Panel Study of Income Dynamics (PSID). See Arthur C. Brooks, "I Love My Work," *American,* September 17, 2007, accessed January 9, 2015, http://www.aei.org/publication/i-love -my-work/.

11    Author's original calculations; data from the 2002 General Social Survey.

12    Joseph Ratzinger, "Homily of His Eminence Card, Joseph Ratzinger Dean of the College of Cardinals," Vatican, April 18, 2005, accessed March 25, 2015, http://www.vatican.va/gpII/documents/homily-pro-eligendo-pontifice_200 50418_en.html.

13    "Text: George W. Bush's Speech to the NAACP," *Washington Post,* July 10, 2000, accessed March 15, 2015, http://www.washingtonpost.com/wp-srv/on politics/elections/bushtext071000.htm.

14    M. E. P. Seligman, S. F. Maier, and J. Geer, "Alleviation of Learned Helplessness in the Dog," *Journal of Abnormal Psychology* 73, no. 3 (1968): 252–62.

15    Lyn Y. Abramson, Martin E. Seligman, and John D. Teasdale, "Learned Helplessness in Humans: Critique and Reformulation," *Journal of Abnormal Psychology* 87, no. 1 (February 1978): 49–74.

## Chapter 4: Lessons from an Indian Slum and an Austrian Ghost Town

1    Lakshmi Iyer, John D. Macomber, and Namrata Arora, "Dharavi: Developing Asia's Largest Slum," Harvard Business School Case 710-004 (July 2009), accessed February 21, 2015, http://www.artdurnev.com/wp-content/up loads/2010/06/Dharavi.pdf.

2    "Highlights of Annual 2013 Characteristics of New Housing," U.S. Census Bureau (2013), accessed March 11, 2015, https://www.census.gov/con struction/chars/highlights.html.

3    "A Flourishing Slum," *Economist*, December 19, 2007, accessed January 5, 2015, http://www.economist.com/node/10311293.

4    Josephine d'Allant, "Giving the Urban Poor Access to City Centers," *Huffington Post*, December 6, 2013, accessed January 18, 2015, http://www.huffing tonpost.com/josephine-dallant/giving-the-urban-poor-acc_b_4392762.html.

5    Data from the World Bank's "Country Dashboard" tool, accessed March 30, 2015, http://povertydata.worldbank.org/poverty/country/IND.

6    Sadanand Dhume, "Debating the Tiger's Rise," *Wall Street Journal*, April 15, 2013, accessed January 16, 2015, http://www.wsj.com/articles/SB10001 42412788732410090457840483241013390.

7    "GNI Per Capita," World Bank, accessed March 30, 2015, http://data .worldbank.org/indicator/NY.GNP.PCAP.CD/countries/IN?display=graph.

8    Thomas Kostigen, "Recycling Profits," *Market Watch*, November 26, 2007, accessed January 15, 2015, http://www.marketwatch.com/story/in-indias -recycling-capital-10-a-month-brings-hope.

9    Jim Yardley, "In One Slum, Misery, Work, Politics and Hope," *New York Times*, December 28, 2011, accessed January 2, 2015, http://www.nytimes .com/2011/12/29/world/asia/in-indian-slum-misery-work-politics-and-hope .html.

10    Iyer, Macomber, and Arora, "Dharavi."

11    Marie Jahoda, Paul F. Lazarsfeld, Hans Zeisel, and Christian Fleck, *Marienthal: The Sociography of an Unemployed Community* (Chicago: Aldine Atherton, 2002).

12    Carmen Perez-Lanzac, "La Apatía de un 'Nini,'" *El Pais*, November 2, 2014, accessed January 16, 2015, http://politica.elpais.com/politica/2014/10/22 /actualidad/1413974500_362946.html.

13    Pilar Alvarez, "El Paro de los Titulados Españoles Triplica la Media de la OCDE," *El Pais*, September 9, 2014, accessed January 16, 2015, http://sociedad .elpais.com/sociedad/2014/09/09/actualidad/1410246577_609240.html.

14    2007 World Values Survey.

15    Marta Domínguez-Folgueras and Teresa Castro-Martín, "Women's Changing Socioeconomic Position and Union Formation in Spain and Portugal," *Demographic Research* 19, no. 41 (2008), doi:10.4054/DemRes.2008.19.41.

16    "Spain Unemployment Rate," Trading Economics, accessed March 29, 2015, http://www.tradingeconomics.com/spain/unemployment-rate.

17    Pope Francis, "Address of Pope Francis to the European Parliament," Strasbourg, France, November 25, 2014, accessed February 10, 2015, http://w2.vatican.va/content/francesco/en/speeches/2014/november/documents/papa-francesco_20141125_strasburgo-parlamento-europeo.html.

18    Keith Fournier, "Evangelical, Missionary Pope Francis Calls Europe to Return to Jesus Christ and Christian Roots," *Catholic Online*, November 27, 2014, accessed February 5, 2015, http://www.catholic.org/news/international/europe/story.php?id=57785.

19    Robert Manchin, "Religion in Europe: Trust Not Filling the Pews," Gallup, September 21, 2004, accessed March 2, 2015, http://www.gallup.com/poll/13117/religion-europe-trust-filling-pews.aspx.

20    "Everything You Need to Know About Ireland's Disaffected Catholics," *Week*, June 28, 2014, accessed February 5, 2015, http://theweek.com/article/index/263824/everything-you-need-to-know-about-irelands-disaffected-catholics.

21    "French Birth Rate Falls Below Two Children Per Woman," Reuters, January 14, 2014, accessed January 3, 2015, http://www.reuters.com/article/2014/01/14/france-demographics-idUSL6N0KO2FS20140114.

22    Molly Moore, "As Europe Grows Grayer, France Devises a Baby Boom," *Washington Post*, October 18, 2006, accessed January 26, 2015, http://www.washingtonpost.com/wp-dyn/content/article/2006/10/17/AR2006101701652.html.

23    Cassie Werber, "Danes Have Promised Their Government to Have More Sex," Quartz, January 14, 2015, accessed January 29, 2015, http://qz.com/326741/danes-have-promised-their-government-to-have-more-sex/.

24    Data from the U.S. Census Bureau's International Data Base, retrieved March 30, 2015, http://www.census.gov/population/international/data/idb/region.php?N=%20Results%20&T=15&A=both&RT=0&Y=2010,2030&R=-1&C=CA,MX,US.

25    Johns Hopkins Comparative Nonprofit Sector Project, accessed May 17, 2006, http://www.jhu.edu/cnp.

26    Matt Moffett, "Catalan Hamlet Thumbs Nose at Authorities in Madrid by Flying Tiny Spanish Flag," *Wall Street Journal*, November 2, 2014, accessed February 6, 2015, http://www.wsj.com/articles/can-you-see-this-spanish-flag-secessionists-in-spain-thwart-the-banner-police-1414985402.

27    William Harms, "NORC: Americans, Venezuelans Most Proud," *University of Chicago Chronicle* 25, no. 11 (March 2, 2006), accessed March 29, 2015, http://chronicle.uchicago.edu/060302/norc.shtml.

28    Tom W. Smith and Seokho Kim, "National Pride in Cross-National and Temporal Perspective," *International Journal of Public Opinion Research* 18 (Spring 2006): 127–36.

29    Steve Moore, "Under Obama: One Million More Americans Have Dropped Out of Work Force Than Have Found a Job," *Forbes*, October 6, 2014, accessed January 27, 2015, http://www.forbes.com/sites/stevemoore/2014/10/06/under-obama-one-million-more-americans-have-dropped-out-of-work-force-than-have-found-a-job/.

30    "International Comparisons of Annual Labor Force Statistics, 1970–2012," Bureau of Labor Statistics, June 7, 2013, accessed January 8, 2015, http://www.bls.gov/fls/flscomparelf.htm#chart05, table #4.

31    "United States Youth Unemployment Rate," Trading Economics, accessed March 2, 2015, http://www.tradingeconomics.com/united-states/youth-unemployment-rate. Data from U.S. Bureau of Labor Statistics.

32    "Youth Unemployment Rate in EU Member States," Statista, accessed September 20, 2014, http://www.statista.com/statistics/266228/youth-unemployment-rate-in-eu-countries/.

33    "EU Elections: Anti-Immigrant Wave Sweeps Europe," *International Business Times*, May 26, 2014, accessed August 7, 2014, http://www.ibtimes.com/eu-elections-anti-immigrant-wave-sweeps-europe-1590035.

34    Cas Muddle, "The Far Right in the 2014 European Elections: Of Earthquakes, Cartels and Designer Fascists," Monkey Cage blog, *Washington Post*, May 30, 2014, accessed January 20, 2015, http://www.washingtonpost.com/blogs/monkey-cage/wp/2014/05/30/the-far-right-in-the-2014-european-elections-of-earthquakes-cartels-and-designer-fascists/.

35    Richard Wike, "In Europe, Sentiment Against Immigrants, Minorities Runs High," Pew Research Center, May 14, 2014, accessed January 18, 2015, http://www.pewresearch.org/fact-tank/2014/05/14/in-europe-sentiment-against-immigrants-minorities-runs-high/.

36    "Biden to Women: Thanks to ObamaCare, You Can Quit Working," Fox News, accessed February 3, 2015, http://www.foxnews.com/politics/2014/02/27/biden-to-women-thanks-to-obamacare-can-quit-working/.

37    Jim Yardley, "In One Slum, Misery, Work, Politics and Hope," *New York Times*, December 28, 2011, accessed January 2, 2015, http://www.nytimes.com/2011/12/29/world/asia/in-indian-slum-misery-work-politics-and-hope.html.

38    Keith Fournier, "Evangelical, Missionary Pope Francis Calls Europe to Return to Jesus Christ and Christian Roots," *Catholic Online*, November 27,

2014, accessed February 5, 2015, http://www.catholic.org/news/international /europe/story.php?id=57785.

## Chapter 5: A Conservative Social Justice Agenda

1    "Untangling African Hairbraiders from Utah's Cosmetology Regime," video, Institute for Justice, transcript accessed March 20, 2015, http://tran scriptvids.com/v/2tjTheDqQrw.html.

2    Jacob Goldstein, "So You Think You Can Be a Hair Braider?" *New York Times*, June 12, 2012, accessed January 26, 2015, http://www.nytimes .com/2012/06/17/magazine/so-you-think-you-can-be-a-hair-braider.html.

3    "Brushing Out Utah's African Hairbraiding Laws," Institute for Justice, accessed January 25, 2015, http://www.ij.org/utah-hairbraiding-background.

4    Dennis Romboy, "Court Sides with Woman in Hair Braiding Case," KSL .com, August 10, 2012, accessed January 25, 2015, http://www.ksl.com/?sid =21638994.

5    "Real Estate Legislation and Regulations," District of Columbia Department of Consumer and Regulatory Affairs (April 2013), accessed August 24, 2014, http://www.asisvcs.com/publications/pdf/660909.pdf.

6    "Application Instructions and Forms for a Cosmetology License in the District of Columbia," Government of the District of Columbia Occupational and Professional Licensing Administration, accessed August 24, 2014, http:// www.asisvcs.com/publications/pdf/670960.pdf.

7    Ron Haskins, "The Myth of the Disappearing Middle Class," *Washington Post*, March 29, 2012, accessed January 21, 2015, http://www.washingtonpost .com/opinions/the-myth-of-the-disappearing-middle-class/2012/03/29/gIQA sXlsjS_story.html.

8    "Advocating to End Child and Family Homelessness: Five Easy Steps," National Center on Family Homelessness, accessed February 3, 2015, http:// www.familyhomelessness.org/media/314.pdf.

9    S. Jay Olshansky, Toni Antonucci, Lisa Berkman, et al., "Differences in Life Expectancy Due to Race and Educational Differences Are Widening, and Many May Not Catch Up," *Health Affairs* 31, no. 8 (August 2012), doi:10.1377 /hlthaff.2011.0746.

10    Anandi Mani, Sendhil Mullainathan, Eldar Shafir, and Jiaying Zhao, "Poverty Impedes Cognitive Function," *Science* 341, no. 6149 (August 2013), doi: 10.1126/science.1238041.

11    Brady Dennis, "Poverty Strains Cognitive Abilities, Opening Door for Bad Decision-Making, New Study Finds," *Washington Post*, August 29, 2013, accessed February 7, 2015, http://www.washingtonpost.com/national/health-science /poverty-strains-cognitive-abilities-opening-door-for-bad-decision-making

-new-study-finds/2013/08/29/89990288-102b-11e3-8cdd-bcdc09410972_story
.html.

12    Przemyslaw Tomalski, Derek G. Moore, Helena Ribeiro, et al., "Socio-economic Status and Functional Brain Development: Associations in Early Infancy," *Developmental Science* 16, no. 5 (September 2013), doi:10.1111/desc .12079.

13    Author's original calculations; data from the 2000 Social Capital Community Benchmark Survey. See Arthur C. Brooks, *Who Really Cares: The Surprising Truth about Compassionate Conservatism* (New York: Basic Books, 2006), 21.

14    Author's original calculations; data from the 2002 General Social Survey. See Brooks, *Who Really Cares*, 22.

15    Giving USA Foundation, *Giving USA 2013: The Annual Report on Philanthropy for the Year 2012*, Indiana University (2013).

16    Katrina total figure from Caroline Preston and Nicole Wallace, "American Donors Gave $1.4 Billion to Haiti Aid," *Chronicle of Philanthropy*, January 6, 2011, accessed March 28, 2015, https://philanthropy.com/article /Haiti-Aid-Falls-Short-of-Other/159311. Comparison to September 11 donations from Thomas Frank, "Katrina Inspires Record Charity," *USA Today*, November 13, 2005.

17    I use the National Hurricane Center's "total damage estimate" of $108 billion. See Richard D. Knabb, Jamie R. Rhome, and Daniel P. Brown, "Tropical Cyclone Report: Hurricane Katrina," National Hurricane Center, last updated August 10, 2006, accessed March 29, 2015, http://www.nhc.noaa.gov/pdf/TCR -AL122005_Katrina.pdf.

18    F. A. Hayek, *The Road to Serfdom*, edited by Bruce Caldwell (Chicago: University of Chicago Press, 2007), 148.

19    Ronald Reagan, Inaugural Address, January 5, 1967, retrieved on March 24, 2015, http://reagan.convio.net/site/DocServer/ReaganMomentsFeb _-_4_-_Inaugural_Address_1967_-_Governor.pdf?docID=584.

20    Francis, "Address of Pope Francis to the Participants in the World Meeting of Popular Movements," Vatican, October 28, 2014, accessed March 3, 2015, https://w2.vatican.va/content/francesco/en/speeches/2014/october/documents /papa-francesco_20141028_incontro-mondiale-movimenti-popolari.html.

21    Ashley N. Edwards, "Dynamics of Economic Well-Being: Poverty, 2009–2011," U.S. Census Bureau (January 2014), accessed September 22, 2014, http:// www.census.gov/content/dam/Census/library/publications/2014/demo/p70 -137.pdf.

22    Christopher Matthews, "Nearly Half of America Lives Paycheck-to-Paycheck," *Time*, January 30, 2014, accessed March 30, 2015, http://time.com /2742/nearly-half-of-america-lives-paycheck-to-paycheck/.

23    Niki Kitsantonis, "Public Suicide for Greek Man with Fiscal Woe," *New York Times*, April 4, 2012, accessed November 16, 2014, http://www.nytimes .com/2012/04/05/world/europe/greek-man-ends-financial-despair-with-bullet .html.

24    "A Hard Subject for a Sermon," Erasmus blog, *Economist*, October 21, 2013, accessed March 1, 2015, http://www.economist.com/blogs/erasmus/2013/10 /greece-and-suicide.

25    Andrew Coulson, "Chart of the Day: Federal Ed Spending," Cato Institute, September 30, 2009, accessed January 30, 2015, http://www.cato.org/blog /chart-day-federal-ed-spending.

26    "2014 District of Columbia Comprehensive Assessment System Results," Office of the State Superintendent of Education, July 31, 2014, accessed February 12, 2015, http://osse.dc.gov/sites/default/files/dc/sites/osse/publication /attachments/2014%20DC%20CAS%20Result%20July%2031%202014...FINAL _.pdf.

27    Matthew M. Chingos and Paul E. Peterson, "The Effects of School Vouchers on College Enrollment: Experimental Evidence from New York City," Brown Center on Education Policy at Brookings and Harvard's Program on Education Policy and Governance (August 2012), accessed April 7, 2014, http:// www.hks.harvard.edu/pepg/PDF/Impacts_of_School_Vouchers_FINAL.pdf.

28    Caroline M. Hoxby, Sonali Murarka, and Jenny Kang, "How New York City's Charter Schools Affect Achievement," New York City Charter Schools Evaluation Project (September 2009), accessed April 7, 2014, http://users.nber.org /~schools/charterschoolseval/how_NYC_charter_schools_affect_achieve ment_sept2009.pdf.

29    Joshua D. Angrist, Sarah R. Cohodes, Susan M. Dynarski, et al., "Student Achievement in Massachusetts' Charter Schools," Center for Education Policy Research at Harvard University (January 2011), accessed March 24, 2015, http:// economics.mit.edu/files/6493.

30    Frederick Hess, "Does School Choice 'Work'?" *National Affairs* 5 (Fall 2010), accessed March 4, 2015, http://www.nationalaffairs.com/publications /detail/does-school-choice-work.

31    Roland G. Fryer, Jr., Steven D. Levitt, John List, et al., "Enhancing the Efficacy of Teacher Incentives Through Loss Aversion: A Field Experiment," NBER Working Paper No. 18237 (July 2012), doi:10.3386/w18237.

32    Number of teachers in California retrieved from "Fingertip Facts on Education in California," California Department of Education, accessed March 14, 2015, http://www.cde.ca.gov/ds/sd/cb/ceffingertipfacts.asp. Number of administrators retrieved from a custom report generated by the California Department of Education's "Dataquest" tool, accessed March 14, 2015, http://dq.cde .ca.gov/dataquest/. Budgetary information retrieved from "Education Budget," California Department of Education, accessed March 14, 2015, http://www.cde

.ca.gov/fg/fr/eb/cefedbudget.asp and "General Fund Budget Summary," California Department of Education, accessed March 14, 2015, http://www.cde.ca.gov/fg/fr/eb/gbudsum14.asp.

33 National Center for Education Statistics, *Digest of Education Statistics, 2012*, U.S. Department of Education (2013), ch. 3, accessed December 2, 2014, http://nces.ed.gov/fastfacts/display.asp?id=76.

34 Ibid.

35 Danielle Kurtzleben, "Just How Fast Has College Tuition Grown?" *U.S. News & World Report*, October 23, 2013, accessed March 12, 2015, http://www.usnews.com/news/articles/2013/10/23/charts-just-how-fast-has-college-tuition-grown.

36 Kevin Kiley, "A 10,000 Platform," *Inside Higher Ed*, November 30, 2012, accessed March 26, 2015, https://www.insidehighered.com/news/2012/11/30/texas-florida-and-wisconsin-governors-see-large-overlap-higher-education-platforms.

37 Darryl Tippens, "Technology Has Its Place: Behind a Caring Teacher," *Chronicle of Higher Education*, August 6, 2012, accessed March 2, 2015, http://chronicle.com/article/Technology-Has-Its-Place-/133329/.

38 Kiley, "A $10,000 Platform."

39 Jim Clifton, "American Entrepreneurship: Dead or Alive," Gallup, January 12, 2015, accessed March 3, 2015, http://www.gallup.com/businessjournal/180431/american-entrepreneurship-dead-alive.aspx.

40 Carmen DeNavas-Walt and Bernadette D. Proctor, "Current Population Reports, P60-249, Income and Poverty in the United States: 2013," U.S. Census Bureau (2014), accessed March 6, 2015, http://www.census.gov/content/dam/Census/library/publications/2014/demo/p60-249.pdf.

41 Rebecca Rifkin, "In U.S., 67% Dissatisfied with Income, Wealth Distribution," Gallup, January 20, 2014, accessed March 27, 2015, http://www.gallup.com/poll/166904/dissatisfied-income-wealth-distribution.aspx.

42 Jeffrey Clemens and Michael Wither, "The Minimum Wage and the Great Recession: Evidence of Effects on the Employment and Income Trajectories of Low-Skilled Workers," NBER Working Paper No. 20724 (December 2014), doi:10.3386/w20724.

43 Michael Strain, "More than the Minimum Wage," *National Review Online*, December 11, 2013, accessed March 2, 2015, http://www.nationalreview.com/article/365999/more-minimum-wage-michael-r-strain.

44 "Higher Pay? Some Disabled Say No Thanks as U.S. Forces It," Bloomberg Business, October 23, 2014, accessed February 14, 2015, http://www.bloomberg.com/news/articles/2014-10-23/higher-pay-some-disabled-say-no-thanks-as-u-s-forces-it.

45    Bureau of Labor Statistics, "Employment Status of the Civilian Population by Race, Age, and Sex February 2014-February 2015," U.S. Department of Labor, last modified March 6, 2015, accessed March 12, 2015, http://www.bls.gov/news.release/empsit.t02.htm.

46    Bureau of Labor Statistics, "Unemployment Rates for Metropolitan Areas—January 2015," U.S. Department of Labor, last modified March 20, 2015, accessed March 27, 2015, http://www.bls.gov/web/metro/laummtrk.htm.

## Chapter 6: From Protest Movement to Social Movement

1    Tom Blumer, "Rant for the Ages: CNBC's Rick Santelli Goes Off; Studio Hosts Invoke 'Mob Rule' to Downplay," blog posting, NewsBusters, February 19, 2009, accessed January 14, 2015, http://newsbusters.org/blogs/tom-blumer/2009/02/19/rant-ages-cnbcs-rick-santelli-goes-studio-hosts-invoke-mob-rule-downplay.

2    "Unusually Wide Gap in 'Satisfaction,' 'Right Direction' Measures," Pew Research Center, March 26, 2009, accessed February 9, 2015, http://www.pewresearch.org/2009/03/26/unusually-wide-gap-in-satisfaction-right-direction-measures/.

3    "GOP roars back to take U.S. House; Democrats cling to Senate majority," CNN, November 3, 2010, accessed March 13, 2015, http://www.cnn.com/2010/POLITICS/11/02/election.main/.

4    Jeffrey M. Jones, "Record High in U.S. Say Big Government Greatest Threat," Gallup, December 18, 2013, accessed January 22, 2015, http://www.gallup.com/poll/166535/record-high-say-big-government-greatest-threat.aspx.

5    "Tea Party Movement," Gallup, accessed February 21, 2015, http://www.gallup.com/poll/147635/tea-party-movement.aspx.

6    There is an enormous literature in sociology on social movements. I don't pretend here to represent it comprehensively, and some sociologists might dispute the steps I delineate between protest and social movements. However, I believe my approach is consistent with canonical descriptions such as that of Herbert G. Blumer. In his words, "Social movements can be viewed as collective enterprises to establish a new order of life. They have their inception in the condition of unrest, and derive their motive power on one hand from dissatisfaction with the current form of life, and on the other hand, from wishes and hopes for a new scheme or system of living." Herbert G. Blumer, "Collective Behavior," in *An Outline of the Principles of Sociology*, edited by Robert E. Park (New York: Barnes & Noble, 1939), 199.

7    Martin Luther King Jr., "I Have a Dream," American Rhetoric, accessed February 8, 2015, http://www.americanrhetoric.com/speeches/mlkihaveadream.htm.

8    Lydia Saad, "On King Holiday, a Split Review of Civil Rights Progress," Gallup, January 21, 2008, accessed January 9, 2015, http://www.gallup.com /poll/103828/civil-rights-progress-seen-more.aspx.

9    Frank Newport, David W. Moore, and Lydia Saad, "Long-Term Gallup Poll Trends: A Portrait of American Public Opinion Through the Century," Gallup, December 20, 1999, accessed February 22, 2015, http://www.gallup .com/poll/3400/longterm-gallup-poll-trends-portrait-american-public -opinion.aspx.

10    David Aberle would distinguish civil rights as a revolutionary social movement, while classifying MADD as a reformative social movement. See David F. Aberle, *The Peyote Religion among the Navaho* (Chicago: Aldine, 1966).

11    "In Honor Of . . . ," Mothers Against Drunk Driving, accessed February 13, 2015, http://www.madd.org/about-us/history/cari-lightner-and-laura -lamb-story.pdf.

12    "25 Years of Saving Lives," Mothers Against Drunk Driving, accessed February 12, 2015, http://www.madd.org/about-us/history/madd25thhistory.pdf.

13    Ibid.

14    "MADD Milestones," Mothers Against Drunk Driving, accessed February 13, 2015, http://www.madd.org/about-us/history/madd-milestones.pdf.

15    Robert M. Calhoon, "Loyalism and Neutrality," in *A Companion to the American Revolution*, edited by Jack P. Greene and J. R. Pole (Oxford: Blackwell, 2003).

## Chapter 7: The Seven Habits of Highly Effective Conservatives

1    M. V. Hood III and Seth McKee, "True Colors: White Conservative Support for Minority Republican Candidates," *Public Opinion Quarterly* (2015), doi:10.1093/poq/nfu057.

2    Devin Dwyer, "Obama: If We Lose in 2012, Government Will Tell People 'You're on Your Own,' " ABC News, October 26, 2011, accessed January 28, 2015, http://abcnews.go.com/blogs/politics/2011/10/obama-if-we-lose-in-2012 -government-will-tell-people-youre-on-your-own/.

3    Ed Pilkington, "Obama Angers Midwest Voters with Guns and Religion Remark," *Guardian*, April 14, 2008, accessed January 15, 2015, http://www .theguardian.com/world/2008/apr/14/barackobama.uselections2008.

4    "The AP-GfK Poll," GfK Public Affairs, accessed December 8, 2014, http://ap-gfkpoll.com/main/wp-content/uploads/2013/10/AP-GfK-October -2013-Poll-Topline-Final_VIEWS.pdf.

5    Lisa Farwell and Bernard Weiner, "Bleeding Hearts and the Heartless: Popular Perceptions of Liberal and Conservative Ideologies," *Personality and Social Psychology Bulletin* 26, no. 7 (September 2000), doi: 10.1177/0146167200269009.

6      Haley Geffen, "The Napkin Doodle That Launched the Supply-Side Revolution," *Bloomberg Business*, December 4, 2014, accessed January 13, 2015, http://www.businessweek.com/articles/2014-12-04/laffer-curve-napkin -doodle-launched-supply-side-economics.

7      "The Effects of a Minimum-Wage Increase on Employment and Family Income," Congressional Budget Office (February 2014), accessed February 10, 2015, https://www.cbo.gov/publication/44995.

8      Lydia Saad, "U.S. Liberals at Record 24%, but Still Trail Conservatives," Gallup, January 9, 2015, accessed February 28, 2015, http://www.gallup.com /poll/180452/liberals-record-trail-conservatives.aspx.

9      See, for example: "iPad Air 2—Change," YouTube video, 1:00, accessed March 1, 2015, https://www.youtube.com/user/Apple?v=ROZhrRm88ms.

10     Kevin Clark, "Andrew Luck: The NFL's Most Perplexing Trash Talker," *Wall Street Journal*, December 16, 2014, accessed January 19, 2015, http:// www.wsj.com/articles/andrew-luck-the-nfls-most-perplexing-trash-talker -1418663249.

11     Danny Hayes, "Candidate Qualities Through a Partisan Lens: A Theory of Trait Ownership," *American Journal of Political Science* 49, no. 4 (October 2005), accessed August 2, 2014, http://home.gwu.edu/~dwh/trait_ownership .pdf.

12     David Mills, "Sister Souljah's Call to Arms: The Rapper Says the Riots Were Payback. Are You Paying Attention?" *Washington Post*, May 13, 1992, accessed January 16, 2015, http://www.washingtonpost.com/wp-dyn/content /article/2010/03/31/AR2010033101709.html.

13     Gwen Ifill, "The 1992 Campaign: Democrats; Clinton at Jackson Meeting: Warmth, and Some Friction," *New York Times*, June 14, 1992, accessed February 23, 2015, http://www.nytimes.com/1992/06/14/us/the-1992-campaign -democrats-clinton-at-jackson-meeting-warmth-and-some-friction.html.

14     "Sister Souljah Moment," C-SPAN video, 2:34, July 28, 2013, accessed November 18, 2014, http://www.c-span.org/video/?c4460582/sister-souljah -moment.

15     Jeffrey Goldberg, "Hillary Clinton: 'Failure' to Help Syrian Rebels Led to the Rise of ISIS," *Atlantic*, August 10, 2014, accessed February 27, 2015, http:// www.theatlantic.com/international/archive/2014/08/hillary-clinton-failure -to-help-syrian-rebels-led-to-the-rise-of-isis/375832/.

16     Interview with Daniela Schiller, December 17, 2014.

17     Daniela Schiller, Jonathan B. Freeman, Jason P. Mitchell, James S. Uleman, and Elizabeth A. Phelps, "A Neural Mechanism of First Impressions," *Nature Neuroscience* 12 (2009), doi:10.1038/nn.2278.

# INDEX

# ABOUT THE AUTHOR

Arthur C. Brooks is president of the American Enterprise Institute, where he is also the Ravenel and Beth Curry Scholar in Free Enterprise. Until 2009, he was the Louis A. Bantle Professor of Business and Government Policy at Syracuse University. Before entering academia, he spent 12 years as a professional French hornist with the City Orchestra of Barcelona and other ensembles. Mr. Brooks is a contributing opinion writer for the *New York Times* and the author of ten books, most recently the 2012 bestseller *The Road to Freedom*. He is a native of Seattle and currently lives in Maryland with his wife, Ester, and their three children.